175 Multiple-Choice Questions in Java™

From
Continental Mathematics League
Contests in Computer Science
1999-2005

Maria Litvin
Phillips Academy, Andover, Massachusetts

Gary Litvin
Skylight Software, Inc.

Skylight Publishing
Andover, Massachusetts

ISBN 0-9727055-1-1

Library of Congress Control Number: 2005901044

Skylight Publishing
9 Bartlet Street, Suite 70
Andover, MA 01810

web: http://www.skylit.com
e-mail: sales@skylit.com
support@skylit.com

1 2 3 4 5 6 7 8 9 10 09 08 07 06 05

Printed in the United States of America

Preface

The Continental Mathematics League has been bringing us fun competitions in mathematics and computer science for many years. The annual CML contest in computer science takes place every spring, shortly before the Advanced Placement exams. It offers 25 challenging multiple-choice questions for 40 minutes. The questions mostly stay within the range of the standard AP CS curriculum, but many of them add an unusual twist or turn, and it is very difficult to answer all of them correctly within the allotted time. With the time limit removed, however, these questions offer a great opportunity to test your knowledge of the subject, fill in gaps, gain new insights, and get "heavy-duty" practice for the AP exam.

The questions from the 1999-2003 contests were published in our earlier book, *125 Multiple-Choice Questions in Java.* Some of these questions were converted into Java from C++; other questions on Java and object-oriented programming, were written specifically for that book. This edition adds questions from the 2004 and 2005 contests. These contests were in Java, and they are presented here without any changes.

Those questions that require knowledge of AB-level topics are marked ^{AB}. The index at the end of the book lists questions by subject area. The questions are based on the Java 1.2 - Java 1.4 releases.

Our sincere thanks to Joseph Quartararo, the president of the Continental Mathematics League, for organizing the National CML Contests in computer science and for his support of this book.

M.L. and G.L.

❖ ❖ ❖

Maria Litvin teaches mathematics and computer science at Phillips Academy in Andover, Massachusetts. She is the author of *C++ for You++* (1998), *Be Prepared for the AP Computer Science Exam* (1999, 2003), *Java Methods: An Introduction to Object-Oriented Programming* (2001), and *Java Methods AB: Data Structures* (2003), all published by Skylight Publishing.

Gary Litvin is the founder of Skylight Software, Inc. and Skylight Publishing. He is the co-author of *C++ for You++* and the *Java Methods* books.

Contents

Directions

Assume that all fragments of code have correct syntax with all required *import* statements present and all variables properly declared, unless stated otherwise.

The following interfaces and classes are used in many questions:*

```
public class ListNode  // represents a node in a linked list
{
  private Object value;
  private ListNode next;

  public ListNode(Object initValue, ListNode initNext)
  {
    value = initValue;
    next = initNext;
  }

  public Object getValue() { return value; }
  public ListNode getNext() { return next; }
  public void setValue(Object theNewValue) { value = theNewValue; }
  public void setNext(ListNode theNewNext) { next = theNewNext; }
}

public class TreeNode  // represents a node in a binary tree
{
  private Object value;
  private TreeNode left;
  private TreeNode right;

  public TreeNode(Object initValue,
                  TreeNode initLeft, TreeNode initRight)
  {
    value = initValue;
    left = initLeft;
    right = initRight;
  }

  public Object getValue() { return value; }
  public TreeNode getLeft() { return left; }
  public TreeNode getRight() { return right; }
  public void setValue(Object theNewValue) { value = theNewValue; }
  public void setLeft(TreeNode theNewLeft) { left = theNewLeft; }
  public void setRight(TreeNode theNewRight)
  { right = theNewRight; }
}
```

* Adapted from The College Board's *AP Computer Science AB: Implementation Classes and Interfaces.*

```
public interface Stack
{
  boolean isEmpty();
  void push(Object obj);
  Object pop();
  Object peekTop();
}

public class ArrayStack implements Stack
{
  private java.util.ArrayList array;

  public ArrayStack()  { array = new java.util.ArrayList(); }
  public boolean isEmpty() { return array.size() == 0; }
  public void push(Object obj) { array.add(obj); }
  public Object pop() { return array.remove(array.size() - 1); }
  public Object peekTop() { return array.get(array.size() - 1); }
}

public interface Queue
{
  boolean isEmpty();
  void enqueue(Object obj);
  Object dequeue();
  Object peekFront();
}

public class ListQueue implements Queue
{
  private java.util.LinkedList list;

  public ListQueue() { list = new java.util.LinkedList(); }
  public boolean isEmpty() { return list.size() == 0; }
  public void enqueue(Object obj) { list.addLast(obj); }
  public Object dequeue() { return list.removeFirst(); }
  public Object peekFront() { return list.getFirst(); }
}
```

2005

1. What is the size of a `double` variable in Java?

   (A) 2 bytes
   (B) 4 bytes
   (C) 8 bytes
   (D) It depends on a compiler setting
   (E) It depends on the operating system

2. What is displayed by

```
System.out.println("1" + new Integer(2) + 3);
```

   (A) The statement has a syntax error and won't compile
   (B) `6`
   (C) `15`
   (D) `123`
   (E) `ClassCastException`

3. Which of the following best describes the set of all pairs of values for `boolean` variables *a* and *b*, such that

```
(!a && b) == !(a || b)
```

   evaluates to `true`?

   (A) Empty set
   (B) Only one pair: `a == true, b == false`
   (C) Two pairs in which `a == true`
   (D) Two pairs in which `a != b`
   (E) All four possible combinations of values

4.[AB] When you try to compile `MyClass`, the Java compiler gives an error message

```
MyClass is not abstract and does not override abstract method
< some method > in java.util.Comparator
```

Which of the following is < *some method* > in the error message?

(A) `equals(myClass)`
(B) `compareTo(myClass)`
(C) `compare(myClass, myClass)`
(D) `compareTo(java.lang.Object)`
(E) `compare(java.lang.Object,java.lang.Object)`

5. Consider the following classes:

```
public class Year2005
{
  public String toString() { return "2005"; }
}

public class Test2005 extends Year2005
{
  public void print()
  {
    < missing statement >
  }
}
```

Which of the following could replace < *missing statement* > so that `Test2005` would compile with no errors and

```
Test2005 test = new Test2005();
test.print();
```

would display `2005`?

I. `System.out.println(new Year2005());`

II. `System.out.println(new Test2005());`

III. `System.out.println(this);`

(A) I only
(B) II only
(C) I and II
(D) II and III
(E) I, II, and III

6. What is the value of `a[1]` after the following code is executed?

```
int[] a = {0, 2, 4, 1, 3};
for (int i = 0; i < a.length; i++)
  a[i] = a[(a[i] + 3) % a.length];
```

(A) 0
(B) 1
(C) 2
(D) 3
(E) 4

7. Consider the method

```
public String mystery(String s)
{
  String s1 = s.substring(0, 1);
  String s2 = s.substring(1, s.length() - 1);
  String s3 = s.substring(s.length() - 1);
  if (s.length() <= 3)
    return s3 + s2 + s1;
  else
    return s1 + mystery(s2) + s3;
}
```

What is the output of

```
System.out.println(mystery("DELIVER"));
```

(A) DELIVER
(B) DEVILER
(C) REVILED
(D) RELIVED
(E) DLEIEVR

8.[AB] Consider the following code segment:

```
List list = new LinkedList();
list.add("["); list.add("A"); list.add("]");
System.out.println(list);

ListIterator it = list.listIterator();
while(it.hasNext())
{
  if ("[".equals(it.next()) || "]".equals(it.next()))
    it.remove();
  else
    it.add("*");
}
System.out.println(list);
```

The first output line is

```
[[, A, ]]
```

What is the second output line?

(A) `[A]`
(B) `[A, B]`
(C) `[B, A]`
(D) `ClassCastException`
(E) `NoSuchElementException`

9. Which of the following is not a method of `java.util.ArrayList`?

(A) `add(Object x);`
(B) `remove(Object x);`
(C) `insert(int i, Object x);`
(D) `contains(Object x);`
(E) `set(int i, Object x);`

<u>Questions 10-11</u> refer to

```
public interface InterfaceA { void methodA(); }

public interface InterfaceB extends InterfaceA { void methodB(); }

public class ClassA implements InterfaceA
{
  public void methodA() {}
  public void methodB() {}
}

public class ClassB extends ClassA implements InterfaceB
{
  public ClassB() {}
  ... < methods not shown >
}
```

10. What is the minimum set of methods that must be defined in `classB` for it to compile with no errors?

(A) No particular methods are required
(B) `methodA`
(C) `methodB`
(D) `methodA` and `methodB`
(E) `methodA`, `methodB`, and `toString`

11. Which of the following statements causes a syntax error?

(A) `InterfaceA obj = new ClassA();`
(B) `InterfaceB obj = new ClassA();`
(C) `InterfaceA obj = new ClassB();`
(D) `InterfaceB obj = new ClassB();`
(E) `ClassA obj = new ClassB();`

<u>Questions 12-13</u> refer to the following method `rotate` **that takes a two-dimensional array** `a` **and returns a two-dimensional array** `b` **made by rotating** `a` by 90° counterclockwise:

```
public int[][] rotate(int[][] a)
{
  int rows = < expression 1 >;
  int cols = < expression 2 >;
  int[][] b = < expression 3 >;

  for (int r = 0; r < rows; r++)
    for (int c = 0; c < cols; c++)
      b[r][c] = < expression 4 >;

  return b;
}
```

For example, if `a` holds

```
1 2 3
4 5 6
```

`b = rotate(a)` will hold

```
3 6
2 5
1 4
```

12.[AB] Which of the following should replace < *expression 1* >, < *expression 2* >, and < *expression 3* >?

	< *expression 1* >	< *expression 2* >	< *expression 3* >
(A)	`a.cols`	`a.rows`	`new int(rows, cols)`
(B)	`a.cols`	`a.rows`	`new int[][](rows, cols)`
(C)	`a.cols()`	`a.rows()`	`new int(rows, cols)`
(D)	`a[0].length`	`a.length`	`new int[rows][cols]`
(E)	`a[0].length`	`a.length`	`new int[][](rows, cols)`

13.[AB] Which of the following should replace < *expression 4* >?

(A) `a[c][r]`
(B) `a[c][rows - 1 - r]`
(C) `a[cols - 1 - c][r]`
(D) `a[cols - 1 - c][rows - 1 - r]`
(E) `a[rows - 1 - r][cols - 1 - c]`

14. What is the value of n after the following code is executed?

```
int n = 2005;
for (int i = 0; i < 50; i++)
  n = (n + 3) / 2;
```

(A) 0
(B) 1
(C) 2
(D) 3
(E) 65

15. What is the output of the following code segment?

```
List cities = new ArrayList();
cities.add("Atlanta");
cities.add("Boston");

for (int i = 1; i < cities.size(); i++)
  cities.add(i, "+");

System.out.println(cities);
```

(A) `[Atlanta, Boston]`
(B) `[Atlanta, +, Boston]`
(C) `[Atlanta, Boston, +]`
(D) `[Atlanta, +, Boston, +]`
(E) No output because the program goes into an infinite loop

16. Which of the following statements is true?

(A) A static variable cannot be initialized in a constructor.
(B) A static variable must be declared final.
(C) An instance variable can't be declared final.
(D) A static method can't access an instance variable.
(E) Only a static method can access a static variable.

17.[AB] a and b are arrays of integers and each of them has n elements. a is sorted in ascending order and b is sorted in descending order. What is the big-O, in terms of n, for the number of comparisons in an optimal algorithm that determines whether there exists i, such that $a[i] == b[i]$?

(A) $O(\log n)$
(B) $O((\log n)^2)$
(C) $O(n)$
(D) $O(n \log n)$
(E) $O(n^2)$

18.[AB] What is the output of the following code?

```
String key = "";
Map map = new TreeMap();
for (int k = 0; k < 3; k++)
{
  key += k;
  String value = "A";
  map.put(key, value);
  value += "B";
  map.put(key, value);
}
System.out.println(map.size());
```

(A) 1
(B) 2
(C) 3
(D) 4
(E) 6

19.[AB] Consider the following method:

```
private TreeNode mysteryProcess(TreeNode root)
{
  if (root == null ||
            (root.getLeft() == null && root.getRight() == null))
    return null;
  else
  {
    root.setLeft(mysteryProcess(root.getLeft()));
    root.setRight(mysteryProcess(root.getRight()));
    return root;
  }
}
```

If `root` refers to the root of the tree

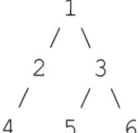

```
     1
    / \
   2   3
  /   / \
 4   5   6
```

which of the following trees is returned by `mysteryProcess(root)`?

(A)
```
1
```

(B)
```
1
 \
  3
```

(C)
```
   1
  / \
 2   3
```

(D)
```
     1
    / \
   2   3
  /
 4
```

(E)
```
1
 \
  3
 / \
5   6
```

20.[AB] What is the output of the following code?

```
Stack stk = new ArrayStack();
stk.push("A");
stk.push("B");
stk.push(stk);
while (!stk.isEmpty())
{
  Object obj = stk.pop();
  if (obj instanceof Stack)
  {
    while (!((Stack)obj).isEmpty())
      System.out.print(((Stack)obj).pop());
  }
  else
    System.out.print(obj);
}
```

(A) `BA`
(B) `ABBA`
(C) `BAAB`
(D) `BABA`
(E) `ClassCastException`

21.[AB] A priority queue is represented as a minimum heap, stored in an array. When a node is added to the heap, it is first added at the leftmost vacant spot in the current level (or, if the current level is full, at the leftmost spot in the next level), and then the reheap-up procedure is applied. What is the order of values in the array after `"M"`, `"A"`, `"N"`, `"G"`, `"O"`, `"E"`, `"S"` are added to the queue (in this order)?

(A) `A E G M N O S`
(B) `A G E M O N S`
(C) `A E G M N O S`
(D) `A E G S O M N`
(E) `A G E S N O M`

22.[AB] Suppose an array of n elements is sorted in ascending order. Then 5 elements are picked randomly and assigned random values. Which of the following sorting algorithms guarantees to restore the ascending order in that array using no more than $O(n)$ comparisons?

I. Selection Sort II. Insertion Sort III. Mergesort

(A) I only
(B) II only
(C) I and II
(D) II and III
(E) I, II, and III

23. For any object `obj`, a call `obj.getClass().getName()` returns the name of `obj`'s class.

Suppose

```
System.out.println(new A() + "+" + new B());
```

displays

```
A+B
```

Which of the following implementations would produce that result?

I. Class `A` has a method

```
public String toString() { return "A"; }
```

and class `B` has a method

```
public String toString() { return "B"; }
```

II. Both class `A` and class `B` extend class `X` that has a method

```
public String toString() { return getClass().getName(); }
```

III. Both class `A` and class `B` extend an abstract class `X` that has methods

```
public abstract String getName();
public String toString() { return getName(); }
```

Class `A` has a method

```
public String getName() { return "A"; };
```

and class `B` has a method

```
public String getName() { return "B"; };
```

(A) I only
(B) II only
(C) I and II
(D) II and III
(E) I, II, and III

24.[AB] Consider the following class:

```
public class Widget implements Comparable
{
  private int nuts, bolts;

  public Widget(int nuts, int bolts)
        { this.nuts = nuts; this.bolts = bolts; }

  public int compareTo(Object other)
        { return nuts - ((Widget)other).nuts; }

  public boolean equals(Object other)
        { return bolts == ((Widget)other).bolts; }

  public int hashCode() { return bolts; }

  public String toString() { return ""+ nuts; }
}
```

Suppose a non-empty `List list` holds several `Widget` objects and the following statements have been executed:

```
Collections.sort(list);
System.out.println(list);
Set tSet = new TreeSet(list);
Set hSet = new HashSet(list);
```

Which of the following statements is NOT necessarily true?

(A) `tSet.size() <= list.size()`
(B) `hSet.size() <= list.size()`
(C) `hSet.size() == tSet.size()`
(D) `tSet.contains(list.get(list.size() - 1))` returns `true`
(E) The output lists the values of `nuts` in `Widget` objects in `list` in ascending order

25. A multiple-choice test has 25 questions, each with five answer choices, A - E. On the eve of the test, Casey and other students had learned that the correct answers on the test were not balanced properly: 3 correct answers were C, 7 were D, and 15 were E (A and B were never correct answers). Casey spent the rest of the night devising an optimal strategy for using this information (neglecting to review the test material). In the worst case, how many questions is Casey guaranteed to get right using the optimal strategy?

(A) 3
(B) 5
(C) 7
(D) 10
(E) 15

2004

1. `twist` is defined as follows:

```
public void twist(String[] w)
{
  String temp = w[0].substring(0, 1);
  w[0] = w[1].substring(0, 1) + w[0].substring(1);
  w[1] = temp + w[1].substring(1);
}
```

What is the output of the following code segment?

```
String[] words = {"HOW", "NEAT"};
twist(words);
System.out.println(words[0] + " " + words[1]);
```

(A) `NOW NOW`
(B) `HOW HOW`
(C) `NOW HOW`
(D) `HOW NEAT`
(E) `NOW HEAT`

2. If `Crossword` extends `Puzzle` and implements `Solvable`, and

```
Puzzle p = new Puzzle();
Crossword cw = new Crossword(10, 20);
```

are declared, which of the following statements will cause a syntax error?

(A) `p = cw;`
(B) `cw = new Puzzle();`
(C) `p = new Crossword(10, 20);`
(D) `Solvable x = new Crossword(10, 20);`
(E) All of the above will compile with no errors.

3. What is the output of the following code?

```
List nums = new ArrayList(3);
nums.add(new Integer(1));
nums.add(new Integer(2));
nums.add(0, nums.get(1));

Object x = nums.get(0);
Object y = nums.get(2);

if (x == y)
  System.out.println(x + " is equal to " + y);
else
  System.out.println(x + " is NOT equal to " + y);
```

(A) `1 is equal to 2`
(B) `1 is NOT equal to 2`
(C) `2 is equal to 2`
(D) `2 is NOT equal to 2`
(E) `IndexOutOfBoundsException`

4.[AB] Which of the following best describes the loop invariant in the following code?

```
double x = 3.0, y = 1.0;
while (x - y > 0.01)
{
  x = (x + y) / 2;
  y = 3.0 / x;
}
```

(A) 3
(B) $x = 3$
(C) $xy = 3$
(D) $xy = 3$ and $x - y > 0.01$
(E) $x = 1.7321428571428572$

5. What is the output of the following code?

```
int sum = 0, p = 1;
for (int count = 1; count <= 50; count++)
{
  sum += p;
  p *= 2;
}
System.out.println(sum);
```

(A) `-1`
(B) `562949953421311` $(= 2^{49} - 1)$
(C) `1125899906842623` $(= 2^{50} - 1)$
(D) `ArithmeticException`
(E) `IllegalArgumentException`

6. What is the output of the following code?

```
String barb = "BARBARA";
scramble(barb);
System.out.println(barb);
```

The method `scramble` is defined as follows:

```
public String scramble(String str)
{
  if (str.length() >= 2)
  {
    int n = str.length() / 2;
    str = scramble(str.substring(n)) + str.substring(0, n);
  }
  return str;
}
```

(A) BARBARA
(B) ARBABAR
(C) AABAR
(D) ARBABARB
(E) ARABARBARB

7. What are the values in `arr` after the following statements are executed?

```
int[] arr = {1, 1, 0, 0, 0};

for (int i = 2; i < arr.length; i++)
  arr[i] += arr[i-1] + arr[i-2];
```

(A) 1 1 0 1 1
(B) 1 1 2 1 0
(C) 1 1 2 2 2
(D) 1 1 2 3 5
(E) 1 1 2 4 8

8. Given

```
double x = 5, y = 2;
```

what is the value of `m` after the following statement is executed?

```
int m = (int)(x + y + x / y - x * y - x / (10*y));
```

(A) -1
(B) -0.75
(C) -0.5
(D) 0
(E) 1

9. What is the value of `sum` after the following code segment is executed?

```
int p = 3, q = 1, sum = 0;
while (p <= 10)
{
  sum += p % q;
  p++;
  q++;
}
```

(A) 0
(B) 10
(C) 12
(D) 14
(E) 52

10.[AB] What is the output of the following code segment?

```
List words = new LinkedList();
int k;

for (k = 1; k <= 9; k++)
  words.add("word" + k);

for (k = 1; k <= words.size(); k++)
  if (k % 3 == 0)
    words.remove(k);

System.out.println(words);
```

(A) `[word1, word2, word4, word5, word7, word8]`
(B) `[word2, word3, word5, word6, word7, word8]`
(C) `[word2, word3, word5, word6, word8, word9]`
(D) `[word1, word2, word3, word5, word6, word7, word9]`
(E) `[word1, word2, word3, word5, word6, word8, word9]`

11. A class `Particle` has a private field `double velocity` and public methods `double getVelocity()` and `void setVelocity(double v)`. It also has a method

```
public void hit(Particle p) { < Missing statements > }
```

Which of the following could replace < *Missing statements* > in `hit` to make it compile with no errors?

I.
```
double v = getVelocity();
setVelocity(p.getVelocity());
p.setVelocity(v);
```

II.
```
double v = velocity;
velocity = p.getVelocity();
p.setVelocity(v);
```

III.
```
double v = velocity;
velocity = p.velocity;
p.velocity = v;
```

(A) I only
(B) II only
(C) I and II
(D) II and III
(E) I, II, and III

12. Which of the following conditions must always be true after the following `while` loop finishes?

```
while (hours < hours0 || (hours == hours0 && mins < mins0))
{
  mins += 5;
  if (mins >= 60)
  {
    mins -= 60;
    hours++;
  }
}
```

(A) `hours > hours0 && mins >= mins0`
(B) `hours >= hours0 && mins >= mins0`
(C) `hours < hours0 || (hours == hours0 && mins < mins0)`
(D) `hours >= hours0 && (hours != hours0 && mins >= mins0)`
(E) `hours >= hours0 && (hours != hours0 || mins >= mins0)`

13. Consider the following class:

```
public class SaleItem implements Comparable
{
  public SaleItem(int p) { price = p; }

  < Comparison method header > { < Code not shown > }

  public String toString() { return String.valueOf(price); }

  private int price;
}
```

Which of the following could replace < *Comparison method header* > to make this class compile with no errors?

I. `public int compare(SaleItem item1, SaleItem item2)`

II. `public boolean compareTo(SaleItem item1)`

III. `public int compareTo(Object obj)`

(A) I only
(B) II only
(C III only
(D) I or II
(E) II or III

<u>Questions 14-15</u> refer to the following classes:

```
public class Gambler
{
  private int money;

  public Gambler(int m) { money = m; }

  public int currentMoney() { return money; }
  public void addMoney(int m) { money += m; }

  public void work() { money += 100 ; }
  public void play() { money /= 2; }
  public void liveAnotherDay() { work(); play(); }

  public String toString() { return String.valueOf(money); }
}

public class CompulsiveGambler extends Gambler
{
  public CompulsiveGambler(int m)
  {
    < Missing statements >
  }

  public void work() { /* do nothing */ }

  public void play()
  {
    while (currentMoney() > 1)
    {
      super.play();
    }
  }
}
```

14. Given that

```
System.out.println(new CompulsiveGambler(300));
```

displays `300`, which of the following could replace < *Missing statements* > in `CompulsiveGambler`'s constructor?

I. `addMoney(m);`

II. `super(m);`

III. `super();`
`addMoney(m);`

(A) I only
(B) II only
(C) I or II
(D) II or III
(E) I, II, or III

15. What is the output of the following code segment?

```
CompulsiveGambler x = new CompulsiveGambler(300);
x.liveAnotherDay();
System.out.println(x);
```

(A) 200
(B) 150
(C) 100
(D) 1
(E) 0

16. Consider the following method:

```
public int goFigure(int x)
{
  if (x < 100)
    x = goFigure(x + 10);
  return (x - 1);
}
```

What does `goFigure(60)` return?

(A) 59
(B) 69
(C) 95
(D) 99
(E) 109

17.[AB] Suppose a `List list` contains strings `"A"`, `"*"`, `"B"`, `"*"`, `"C"` (in this order). What is the output of the following code segment?

```
ListIterator it = list.listIterator();
while (it.hasNext())
{
  if ("*".equals(it.next()))
    it.add(it.next() + "*");
}

System.out.println(list);
```

(A) No output: the program goes into an infinite loop.
(B) `[A, *, **, B, *, **, C]`
(C) `[A, **, *, B, **, *, C]`
(D) `[A, *, B, B*, *, C, C*]`
(E) `[A, *, **, ***, ****, B, *, **, ***, ****, C]`

18.[AB] A linked list pointed to by `ListNode head` contains `Comparable` objects. Which sorting algorithm is implemented by the following method `sort` and its helper method `doSomething`?

```
public ListNode sort(ListNode head)
{
  if (head != null)
    head = doSomething(sort(head.getNext()), head);

  return head;
}

private ListNode doSomething(ListNode head, ListNode node)
{
  if (head == null ||
    ((Comparable)node.getValue()).compareTo(head.getValue()) < 0)
  {
    node.setNext(head);
    head = node;
  }
  else
    head.setNext(doSomething(head.getNext(), node));

  return head;
}
```

(A) Selection Sort
(B) Insertion Sort
(C) Mergesort
(D) Quicksort
(E) Heapsort

19.[AB] A `Map thingsToDo` associates a `Resort` object with a `Set` of activities available at that resort. The following code segment is intended to remove `"Golf"` from the activity sets in all resorts:

```
Iterator iter = thingsToDo.keySet().iterator();
while (iter.hasNext())
  < Missing statement >
```

Which of the following should replace < *Missing statement* >?

(A) `(Set)iter.next().remove("Golf");`
(B) `((Set)iter.next()).remove("Golf");`
(C) `thingsToDo.remove((Set)iter.next(), "Golf");`
(D) `thingsToDo.remove((Resort)iter.next(), "Golf");`
(E) `((Set)thingsToDo.get(iter.next())).remove("Golf");`

20.[AB] What is the output of the following code segment?

```
TreeNode node6 = new TreeNode("6", null, null);
TreeNode node5 = new TreeNode("5", null, null);
TreeNode node4 = new TreeNode("4", null, null);
TreeNode node3 = new TreeNode("3", node5, node6);
TreeNode node2 = new TreeNode("2", null, node4);
TreeNode node1 = new TreeNode("1", node2, node3);
TreeNode root = node1;

Object[] arr = new Object[8];
toArray(root, 1, arr);

for (int i = 0; i <= arr.length - 1; i++)
  System.out.print(arr[i] + " ");
```

The method `toArray` is defined as follows:

```
private void toArray(TreeNode root, int i, Object[] arr)
{
  if (root != null)
  {
    arr[i] = root.getValue();
    toArray(root.getLeft(), 2*i, arr);
    toArray(root.getRight(), 2*i + 1, arr);
  }
}
```

(A) `null 1 2 null 3 4 5 6`
(B) `null 1 2 3 null 4 5 6`
(C) `null 1 2 3 4 null 5 6`
(D) `null 1 2 3 4 5 null 6`
(E) `null 1 2 3 4 5 6 null`

21.[AB] Suppose all valid five-digit zip codes are represented as `Integer` objects and stored in a set containing about 4000 zip codes. Compare two implementations of this set: one is a `HashSet` with 400 buckets; another is a `TreeSet`. Assuming that various zip codes are matched against the set with roughly the same frequency, which of the following statements about the average performance of these implementations is true?

(A) `HashSet` works more than 100 times faster than `TreeSet`.
(B) `HashSet` works about 20 times faster than `TreeSet`.
(C) `HashSet` works 2-4 times faster than `TreeSet`.
(D) `HashSet` works slower than `TreeSet`.
(E) `HashSet` works roughly as fast as `TreeSet`, but takes more than twice as much space.

22.[AB] What is the output of the following code segment?

```
String[] letters = {"A", "B", "C"};
Queue qLetters = new ListQueue();
String sLetters = "";
Stack stk = new ArrayStack();

for (int i = 0; i < letters.length; i++)
{
  qLetters.enqueue(letters[i]);
  stk.push(qLetters);
  sLetters += letters[i];
  stk.push(sLetters);
}
while(!stk.isEmpty())
{
  System.out.print(stk.pop() + " ");
  Queue q = (Queue)stk.pop();
  System.out.print("[");
  while (!q.isEmpty())
    System.out.print(q.dequeue());
  System.out.print("] ");
}
```

(A) `ABC [ABC] AB [] A []`
(B) `ABC [] ABC [] ABC []`
(C) `ABC [ABC] AB [AB] A [A]`
(D) `A [A] AB [AB] ABC [ABC]`
(E) `ClassCastException`

23.[AB] An n by n two-dimensional array contains `Comparable` values. The values in each row are increasing. The columns alternate: in the first, third, and other odd columns the values are increasing and in the second, fourth, and other even columns the values are decreasing. What is the average big-O for an optimal algorithm that finds a given value in such an array?

(A) $O(\log n)$
(B) $O((\log n)^2)$
(C) $O(n)$
(D) $O(n \log n)$
(E) $O(n^2)$

24. Consider the following classes:

```
public abstract class PointXY
{
  private int x, y;

  public PointXY(int x, int y) {this.x = x; this.y = y; }
  public int getX() { return x; }
  public int getY() { return y; }
  public String toString() { return "(" + getX() + "," +
                                        getY() + ")"; }

  public abstract PointXY moveBy(int dx, int dy);
  public abstract double distanceFrom(PointXY p);
}

public abstract class CartesianPoint extends PointXY
{
  public CartesianPoint(int x, int y) {  < Code not shown > }
  public double distanceFrom(PointXY p) { < Code not shown > }
}

public class BoardPosition extends CartesianPoint
{
  < Code not shown >
}
```

Which of the following is the minimal set of public constructors and/or methods required in the `BoardPosition` class, so that the statements

```
BoardPosition pos = new BoardPosition(0, 0);
System.out.println(pos.moveBy(10, 10).distanceFrom(pos));
```

compile and execute with no errors?

(A) `public PointXY moveBy(int dx, int dy)`

(B) `public BoardPosition(int x, int y)` and
`public PointXY moveBy(int dx, int dy)`

(C) `public double distanceFrom(PointXY pos)` and
`public PointXY moveBy(int dx, int dy)`

(D) `public double distanceFrom(BoardPosition pos)` and
`public BoardPosition moveBy(int dx, int dy)`

(E) `public BoardPosition()` and
`public BoardPosition(int x, int y)` and
`public PointXY moveBy(int dx, int dy)`

25. A multiple-choice question deals with the scores that four students received in a contest. The question offers the following answer choices:

a. Tim got more points than Jenny.
b. Tim is the contest winner.
c. Jenny is in last place.
d. Tim's score is above average, and Jenny's score is below average.
e. While Nina did better than Phil, the boys' combined score is higher than the girls' combined score.

The question assumes that one option is true and all the rest are false. But the question is badly designed, making it possible to guess the correct answer from the given choices without even looking at the question. What is the correct answer?

(A) a
(B) b
(C) c
(D) d
(E) e

2003

1. `fun` is defined as follows:

```
public int fun(int[] v)
{
  v[0]--;
  return v[0] + 2;
}
```

What is the value of `v[0]` after the following code segment is executed?

```
int[] v = {3, 4, 5};
v[0] = fun(v);
```

(A) 1
(B) 2
(C) 3
(D) 4
(E) 5

2. The method `xProperty` is defined as follows:

```
public boolean xProperty(int a)
{
  return a == 2 * (a / 10 + a % 10);
}
```

For which of the following values of `a` does `xProperty(a)` return `true`?

(A) 2
(B) 8
(C) 18
(D) 28
(E) 128

3. What are the values of `m` and `n` after the following code runs?

```
int m = 20, n = 2, temp;

for (int count = 1; count <= 20; count++)
{
  temp = m;
  m = n + count;
  n = temp - count;
}
```

(A) $m = 230$ $n = -208$
(B) $m = 30$ $n = -8$
(C) $m = 12$ $n = -10$
(D) $m = -12$ $n = 8$
(E) $m = -190$ $n = 212$

4. Consider the method

```
public int[] copyX(int[] arr)
{
  int[] result = new int[arr.length];

  for (int i = 0; i < arr.length; i++)
  {
    if (arr[i] <= 0)
      break;
    if (arr[i] > 10)
      break;
    result[i] = arr[i];
  }
  return result;
}
```

Suppose it is rewritten as follows:

```
public int[] copyX(int[] arr)
{
  int[] result = new int[arr.length];
  int i = 0;

  while (< condition >)
  {
    result[i] = arr[i];
    i++;
  }
  return result;
}
```

Which of the following expressions can replace < *condition* > so that the second version is equivalent to the first one (i.e., for any `int[]` parameter `arr`, it returns the same result as the first version)?

(A) `i < arr.length && (arr[i] <= 0 || arr[i] > 10)`
(B) `(arr[i] <= 0 || arr[i] > 10) || i >= arr.length`
(C) `(arr[i] > 0 || arr[i] <= 10) && i < arr.length`
(D) `i < arr.length && !(arr[i] <= 0 && arr[i] > 10)`
(E) `i < arr.length && arr[i] > 0 && arr[i] <= 10`

5. Given

```
double x = < any positive value less than 2003 >;
```

which of the following code fragments set `int y` to the smallest integer that is NOT less than three quarters of x?

I.
```
int y = (int)(3 * x / 4);
if (y < 3 * x / 4) y++;
```

II.
```
int y = 1;
while (y < 3 * x / 4) y++;
```

III.
```
int y = 2010 - (int)(2010 - x * 3 / 4);
```

(A) I only
(B) II only
(C) I and II
(D) I and III
(E) I, II, and III

6. Alicia is five years older than her brother Ben. Three years from now Alicia's age will be twice Ben's age. How old are Alicia and Ben now? Hal wrote the following program to solve this puzzle:

```
public class AliciaAndBen
{
  public static void main(String[] args)
  {
    for (int a = 1; a <= 100; a++)
      for (int b = 1; b <= 100; b++)
        if (< condition >)
          System.out.println("Alicia is " + a +
                                            " and Ben is " + b);
  }
}
```

Which of the following expressions should replace `< condition >` in Hal's program so that it displays the correct solution to the puzzle?

(A) `(a == b - 5) && (a - 3 == 2 * (b - 3))`
(B) `a == b + 5 && a + 3 == 2 * b + 6`
(C) `(a == (b + 5)) && ((a + 3) == (2 * b + 3))`
(D) `a == (b - 5) && (2 * a - 3) == (b - 3)`
(E) None of the above works

7.[AB] Suppose a two-dimensional array of `chars` `m` has 4 rows and 5 columns and holds the values represented in the picture below:

```
x.xxx
xx..x
.x.xx
xx...
```

What are the values in `m` after the following code segment is executed?

```
int r, c;
for (r = 1; r < m.length; r++)
  for (c = 1; c < m[0].length - 1; c++)
    if (m[r-1][c-1] == 'x' && m[r-1][c+1] == 'x')
      m[r][c] = 'x';
```

(A)	(B)	(C)	(D)	(E)
x.xxx	xxxxx	xxxxx	x.xxx	x.xxx
xx..x	xx..x	xx.xx	xx.xx	xx.xx
.xxxx	.xxxx	xxxxx	.xxxx	.x.xx
xx...	xx...	xxx..	xxxx.	xxx..

8. What is the output from the following code?

```
String s = "ONION";
System.out.println(
    s.substring(1, 5).substring(1, 4).substring(0, 3));
```

(A) `I`
(B) `IO`
(C) `ION`
(D) `ONI`
(E) `NION`

9. What is the smallest required number of comparisons in an optimal algorithm (based on comparing values) that puts any THREE distinct values into a list in ascending order? What is the answer for FOUR distinct values?

(A) 2 and 3
(B) 3 and 4
(C) 3 and 5
(D) 3 and 6
(E) 6 and 12

10. Given

```
int counts[] = {7, 2, 9, 0, 1, 5, 5, 3, 9};
```

What does `find3(counts, 9)` return? `find3` is defined as follows:

```
public int find3(int a[], int targetSum)
{
  int i = 0, sum = 0;

  while (i < 3)
  {
    sum += a[i];
    i++;
  }

  if (sum == targetSum)
    return 1;

  while (i < a.length)
  {
    sum += a[i] - a[i-3];
    if (sum == targetSum)
      return i - 1;
    i++;
  }
  return -1;
}
```

(A) -1
(B) 1
(C) 2
(D) 3
(E) 8

11.[AB] Let us call an array "oscillating" if its values alternate going up and down, as follows: `a[i-1] < a[i]` and `a[i] > a[i+1]` for any odd i, $0 < i < n-1$, where n is the number of elements in `a`. What is the "big-O" for an optimal algorithm that determines the minimum value in an oscillating array of length n? The median value?

	Minimum	*Median*
(A)	$O(1)$	$O(1)$
(B)	$O(n/2)$	$O(1)$
(C)	$O(n)$	$O(n)$
(D)	$O(n)$	$O(n \log n)$
(E)	$O(n)$	$O(n^2)$

12.[AB] Suppose an n by n matrix of "black" and "white" pixels (e.g., 1s and 0s) represents a picture of a black blob that fills the southeastern corner of the picture. The blob's boundary extends in a generally southwest-to-northeast direction. All the pixels below and to the right of any black pixel are black. For example:

```
0000000
0000001
0000011
0001111
0111111
1111111
1111111
```

What is the worst-case "big-O," in terms of n, for the total number of integer additions plus pixel comparisons in an optimal algorithm that determines the area of a blob (the number of black pixels in the blob)?

(A) $O(\log n)$
(B) $O((\log n)^2)$
(C) $O(n)$
(D) $O(n \log n)$
(E) $O(n^2)$

Questions 13-17 refer to the following interface and classes, written by Kim, a novice programmer, for modeling a "Caller ID" device:

```
public interface Call
{
  String getSource();
}

public class IncomingCall implements Call
{
  private String telephoneNumber;

  public IncomingCall() { telephoneNumber = ""; }
  public IncomingCall(String tel) { telephoneNumber = tel; }

  public void setTelephoneNumber(String tel)
  { telephoneNumber = tel; }

  public String getSource() { return telephoneNumber; }
  public String toString() { return getSource(); }
}

public class IncomingCallWithName extends IncomingCall
{
  private String callerName;

  public IncomingCallWithName(String tel, String name)
  {
    < missing statement >
    callerName = name;
  }

  public String getName() { return callerName; }

  public String getSource()
  { return super.getSource() + " " + getName(); }

  public String toString()
  { return super.getSource() + " " + getName(); }
}
```

13. Kim's teacher specified that

```
System.out.println(
   new IncomingCallWithName("800-749-2000", "Pizza Palace"));
```

should display

```
800-749-2000 Pizza Palace
```

Which of the following statements can replace < *missing statement* > in the `IncomingCallWithName` constructor to achieve that?

I. `super(tel);`
II. `setTelephoneNumber(tel);`
III. `telephoneNumber = tel;`

(A) I only
(B) II only
(C) I and II
(D) II and III
(E) I, II, and III

14. What is the result of the following code segment?

```
Call[] calls = new Call[3];
calls[0] = new IncomingCall("888-888-8888");       // Line 1
calls[1] = (IncomingCallWithName)calls[0];         // Line 2
System.out.println(calls[0] + " " +
                      calls[1] + " " + calls[2]);  // Line 3
```

(A) Syntax error on Line 1
(B) Syntax error on Line 2
(C) `ClassCastException` on Line 2
(D) `NullPointerException` on Line 3
(E) Compiles and runs with no errors; the output is:
`888-888-8888 888-888-8888 null`

15. After correctly completing the `IncomingCallWithName` constructor, as requested in Question 13, Kim wrote the following test code:

```
IncomingCall call =
    new IncomingCallWithName("800-749-2000", "Pizza Palace");
System.out.println(call);
```

The output was

```
800-749-2000 Pizza Palace
```

Kim's teacher suggested that Kim try to compile and run the program again with `IncomingCallWithName`'s `toString` method commented out. What would be the result of this experiment?

(A) Syntax error "IncomingCallWithName should be declared abstract"
(B) Infinite recursion, stack overflow
(C) The program compiles with no errors and displays `800-749-2000`
(D) The program compiles with no errors and displays the same output as before, `800-749-2000 Pizza Palace`
(E) The program compiles with no errors and displays `IncomingCallWithName@47e553`

16. Suppose `calls` and `name` are initialized as follows:

```
Call[] calls = {
  new IncomingCallWithName("800-749-2000", "Pizza Palace"),
  new IncomingCall("888-237-3757"),
  new IncomingCallWithName("800-555-2134", "Burger Heaven")
};

String name = "Pizza Palace";
```

The following code segment is intended to count the number of `Call` objects in the `calls` array that came from a given source:

```
String name = IO.readLine(); // Read the name of the source
int count = 0;
for (int i = 0; i < calls.length; i++)
  if ( < condition > )
    count++;
```

Which of the following replacements for < *condition* > will compile with no errors and correctly set `count` to 1?

(A) `calls[i].getSource().indexOf(name) >= 0`
(B) `calls[i].toString().indexOf(name) >= 0`
(C) `calls[i].getName().equals(name)`
(D) `((IncomingCallWithName)calls[i]).getName().equals(name)`
(E) None of the above

17.[AB] Consider the following class:

```
public class CallerId
{
  private List calls;

  public CallerId()
  {
    calls = new LinkedList();
  }

  // precondition:  calls holds IncomingCall objects
  // postcondition: all calls that came from target are
  //                removed from the calls list
  public void removeAll(String target) { < code not shown > }

  < other methods not shown >
}
```

If `removeAll` works as specified in its pre- and postconditions, which of the following code segments can serve as `removeAll`'s body?

I.

```
for (int i = 0; i < calls.size(); i++)
{
  if (((IncomingCall)calls.get(i)).getSource().equals(target))
    calls.remove(i);
}
```

II.

```
int i = 0;
while (i < calls.size())
{
  if (((IncomingCall)calls.get(i)).getSource().equals(target))
    calls.remove(i);
  else
    i++;
}
```

III.

```
Iterator iter = calls.iterator();
while (iter.hasNext())
{
  if (((IncomingCall)iter.next()).getSource().equals(target))
    iter.remove();
}
```

(A) I only
(B) II only
(C) I and II
(D) II and III
(E) I, II, and III

18.[AB] What is the output of the following code segment?

```
Map m = new TreeMap();
m.put("La", "La");
m.put("La-La", "La");
m.put("La-La-La", "Ye-Ye");
Iterator it = m.keySet().iterator();
while (it.hasNext())
  System.out.print(m.get(it.next()) + " ");
```

(A) `La Ye-Ye`
(B) `La La Ye-Ye`
(C) `La La-La-La`
(D) `La La La-La-La Ye-Ye`
(E) `La La La-La La La-La-La Ye-Ye`

19.[AB] Suppose `ListNode head` refers to the first node of a linked list. Consider the following code fragment:

```
ListNode node, temp;

for (node = head; node != null; node = node.getNext())
{
  while (node.getNext() != null &&
             node.getNext().getValue().equals(node.getValue()))
  {
    node.setNext((node.getNext().getNext()));
  }
}
```

If `head` refers to a linked list with 11 nodes that hold the letters

`"M", "I", "S", "S", "I", "S", "S", "I", "P", "P", "I"`

(in that order), what letters are stored in the nodes of this list after the above code is executed?

(A) `"M"`
(B) `"M", "I", "S"`
(C) `"M", "I", "I", "I", "I"`
(D) `"M", "I", "S", "P"`
(E) `"M ", "I", "S", "I", "S", "I", "P", "I"`

20.[AB] Consider the following method:

```
public int mysteryCount(TreeNode root)
{
  int count = 0;

  if (root != null)
  {
    count = mysteryCount(root.getLeft()) +
            mysteryCount(root.getRight());
    if ((root.getLeft() == null && root.getRight() == null) ||
         (root.getLeft() != null && root.getRight() != null &&
            root.getLeft().getValue().equals(
                                      root.getRight().getValue())))
      count++;
  }
  return count;
}
```

If `root` refers to the tree

```
          A
        /   \
       /     \
      B       C
     / \     /  \
    D   D   C    C
           / \  / \
          E   E E  E
```

which value is returned by `mysteryCount(root)`?

(A) 1
(B) 3
(C) 4
(D) 5
(E) 10

21.[AB] Consider the following method that creates a binary tree from a linked list:

```
public TreeNode listToTree(ListNode head)
{
  if (head == null || head.getNext() == null)
    return null;
  else
    return new TreeNode(head.getValue(),
      listToTree(head.getNext()),
                        listToTree(head.getNext().getNext()));
}
```

If `head` refers to a list with five nodes —

```
"A", "B", "C", "D", "E"
```

— how many nodes in the tree returned by `listToTree(head)` hold `"E"`?

(A) 0
(B) 3
(C) 4
(D) 5
(E) 8

22.[AB] Consider the following method that builds a linked list from a binary tree:

```
public ListNode treeToList(TreeNode root)
{
  if (root == null)
    return null;
  else if (Math.random() < 0.5)
    return new ListNode(root.getValue(),
                           treeToList(root.getLeft()));
  else
    return new ListNode(root.getValue(),
                           treeToList(root.getRight()));
}
```

If `root` refers to the tree

```
       A
      / \
     /   \
    B     C
   / \   /
  D   E F
```

which of the following lists could possibly result from `treeToList(root)`?

I. `A, B, D`
II. `A, B, C, D`
III. `A, C, F`

(A) I only
(B) II only
(C) I and II
(D) I and III
(E) I, II, and III

23.[AB] Consider the following method that builds a binary tree from a queue:

```
// precondition: q holds Comparable objects
public TreeNode queueToTree(ListQueue q)
{
  if (q.isEmpty())
    return null;

  ListQueue q1 = new ListQueue();
  ListQueue q2 = new ListQueue();
  Comparable x, y;

  x = (Comparable)q.dequeue();
  while (!q.isEmpty())
  {
    y = (Comparable)q.dequeue();
    if (y.compareTo(x) < 0)
      q1.enqueue(y);
    else
      q2.enqueue(y);
  }

  return new TreeNode(x, queueToTree(q1), queueToTree(q2));
}
```

If `q` contains letters `A, P, R, I, C, O, T` (represented by `Character` or `String` objects, in this order, from front to rear), what is the result of inorder traversal (left-root-right) of the tree returned by `queueToTree(q)`?

(A) `A, C, I, O, P, R, T`
(B) `A, P, R, T, I, C, O`
(C) `A, P, R, C, I, O, T`
(D) `A, C, O, I, T, R, P`
(E) `A, P, I, C, O, R, T`

24.[AB] Consider the following method `eval`:

```
String eval(Queue q)
{
  Stack stk = new ArrayStack();
  String s = "";

  while (!q.isEmpty())
  {
    s = (String)q.dequeue();

    if (!s.equals("+"))
      stk.push(s);
    else
    {
      String s1 = "", s2 = "";
      if (!stk.isEmpty())
        s2 = (String)stk.pop();
      if (!stk.isEmpty())
        s1 = (String)stk.pop();
      stk.push(s1 + s2);
    }
  }
  if (!stk.isEmpty())
    s = (String)stk.pop();
  return s;
}
```

The program reads strings (which may hold single characters), separated by spaces, one by one from the input line and puts them into a queue `q`. Then it displays the string returned by `eval(q)`. For which of the following input lines is the output `HELLO`?

front
↓

(A) `H + E + L + L + O`
(B) `H E L + + L O + +`
(C) `H E + + L L + O +`
(D) `+ + + + O L L E H`
(E) None of the above

25. A multiple-choice test contains 25 questions. The correct answers include five As, five Bs, five Cs, five Ds, and five Es. Both Constance and Randy solve the first 15 questions correctly but then run out of time. Constance picks the letter (or one of the letters) that is least frequent among the first 15 answers and fills in the remaining 10 answers with this letter. Randy picks random answers for the remaining 10 questions, but he makes sure that at the end each letter A-E appears exactly five times among all 25 answers. Which of the following statements is FALSE?

(A) Randy and Constance can get the same score
(B) Randy's score can be any number from 15 to 25
(C) Constance scores not less than 17
(D) Constance scores not more than 20
(E) Neither Randy nor Constance can score exactly 24

2002

1. If a is an int array of length 2 and a[0] and a[1] hold values 7 and 13 respectively, what are their values after fun(a) is called? The method fun is defined as follows:

```
public void fun(int[] x)
{
  x[0] = (int)(100.0 * x[0] / (x[0] + x[1]));
  x[1] = (int)(100.0 * x[1] / (x[0] + x[1]));
}
```

(A) 7 and 13
(B) 35 and 27
(C) 34 and 64
(D) 35 and 65
(E) 34 and 66

2. Consider a method

```
public boolean isProcessedX(int n, int[] v)
{
  if (n >= 2 && isProcessedX(n-1, v))
  {
    v[n-1] = v[n-2];
    return true;
  }
  else
    return false;
}
```

What happens if an int array s holds values 1, 2, 3, 4, 5 and isProcessedX(5, s) is called?

(A) s holds 1, 2, 3, 4, 5 and isProcessedX returns false
(B) s holds 1, 2, 3, 4, 4 and isProcessedX returns true
(C) s holds 1, 1, 1, 1, 1 and isProcessedX returns true
(D) IndexOutOfBoundsException
(E) Stack overflow error

3. An array `mix` holds seven elements. For which seven values in `mix` will the value of the variable `property` be `true` after the following code segment is executed?

```
int i;
boolean property = true;

for (i = 1; i < 6; i += 2)
{
  if (mix[i] >= mix[i-1] || mix[i] >= mix[i+1])
    property = false;
}
```

(A) 1, 2, 3, 4, 5, 6, 7
(B) 7, 6, 5, 4, 3, 2, 1
(C) 7, 1, 6, 2, 5, 3, 4
(D) 1, 2, 3, 4, 3, 2, 1
(E) 1, 5, 2, 6, 3, 7, 4

4.[AB] The class `Game` has a data member `char[][] board` and a constructor defined as follows:

```
public Game()
{
  board = new char[4][4];
  int r, c;

  for (r = 0; r < 4; r++)
    for (c = 0; c < 4; c++)
      board[r][c] = '.';

  for (r = 0; r < 4; r++)
    board[r][(r + 1) % 4] = 'x';
}
```

What values are stored in `board` when a `Game` object is constructed with the above constructor?

(A)	(B)	(C)	(D)	(E)
`...x`	`..x.`	`...x`	`.x..`	`.x..`
`..x.`	`.x..`	`x...`	`..x.`	`x...`
`.x..`	`x...`	`.x..`	`...x`	`...x`
`x...`	`...x`	`..x.`	`x...`	`..x.`

5. Consider the following method `prepare`:

```
public String prepare(String s)
{
  int k = s.length() / 2;
  if (k <= 1)
    return s;
  return s.charAt(k - 1) +
     prepare(s.substring(0, k - 1) + s.substring(k + 1, 2*k)) +
         s.charAt(k);
}
```

what does `prepare("LEMONADE")` return?

(A) `ONMAEDLE`
(B) `OLEMADEN`
(C) `OMELEDAN`
(D) `OOOONNNN`
(E) `LEMONADE`

6. What are the values of `a` and `b` after the following code fragment is executed?

```
int a = 3, b = 5, s;
for (int i = 0; i < 10; i++)
{
  s = a + b;
  b = a - b;
  a = s;
}
```

(A) 0 and 96
(B) 96 and 0
(C) 96 and 96
(D) 96 and 160
(E) 160 and 96

7. If `int weekDay` contains the code for the day of the week on November 1 (0 for Sunday, 1 for Monday, ..., 6 for Saturday), which of the following expressions gives the date for Thanksgiving (the fourth Thursday in November)?

(A) `weekDay + 26`
(B) `26 - weekDay`
(C) `(4 - weekDay) % 7 + 22`
(D) `(11 - weekDay) % 7 + 22`
(E) `(weekDay + 3) % 7 + 22`

8. The method `average3` below "simultaneously" replaces all elements in an array. Each element is replaced with the average of that element's current value and its left and right neighbors. If a "neighbor" is outside the array, its value is assumed to be 0:

```
public void average3(double a[])
{
  int i, len = a.length;
  double tempSaved[] = new double[len];
  for (i = 0; i < len; i++)
    tempSaved[i] = a[i];

  double leftNeighbor, rightNeighbor;

  for (i = 0; i < len; i++)
  {
    if (i > 0)
      leftNeighbor = tempSaved[i-1];
    else
      leftNeighbor = 0;
    if (i < len - 1)
      rightNeighbor = tempSaved[i+1];
    else
      rightNeighbor = 0;
    a[i] = (leftNeighbor + tempSaved[i] + rightNeighbor) / 3;
  }
}
```

Suppose the first and last elements in `v` are zeroes. Which one of the following statements is FALSE after `average3(v)` is called? (Disregard all inaccuracies that may be introduced due to the floating-point arithmetic.)

(A) If `v` holds the values 0, 3, 6, 9, 12, 9, 6, 3, 0, the resulting array will hold 1, 3, 6, 9, 10, 9, 6, 3, 1.
(B) The sum of all the elements in `v` remains the same.
(C) If in the original array the sum of all the values in even positions, `v[0]+v[2]+...`, is the same as the sum of all the values in the odd positions, `v[1]+v[3]+...`, then the same will remain true for the resulting array.
(D) The maximum value in the resulting array does not exceed the maximum value in the original array.
(E) The position of the maximum element in the resulting array remains the same as in the original array or shifts to one of the two neighboring positions.

9.[AB] An array `arr` contains n integer elements whose values form an arithmetic sequence (i.e., `arr[i+1] - arr[i] == arr[i] - arr[i-1]` for any $0 < i < n-1$). What is the "big-O" for an optimal algorithm that determines whether such an array contains two given values?

(A) $O(1)$
(B) $O(\log n)$
(C) $O(2 \log n)$
(D) $O(n)$
(E) $O(n^2)$

10. Given

```
Random generator = new Random();
int bigNum = 10000;
int r = generator.nextInt(bigNum);
```

which of the following expressions is the best way to initialize `x` to the value of a randomly chosen element from an array `arr` of 3 values? (The odds for choosing any element must be the same or almost the same.)

(A) `x = arr[r / bigNum * 3];`
(B) `x = arr[(int)(3.0 * r / bigNum)];`
(C) `x = arr[(int)(2.9 * r / bigNum)];`
(D) `x = arr[(int)(3.0 * (r - 1) / (bigNum - 1))];`
(E) `x = arr[3 * (int)((double)r / bigNum)];`

11. Given three integer variables, `a`, `b`, and `c`, with small non-negative values, which of the following code fragments tests the condition that any two of the values are zeroes while the third one is positive? The variable `ok` should be set to `true` if and only if the above condition is true.

I.
```
boolean ok =
  a == 0 && b == 0 && c > 0 ||
  b == 0 && c == 0 && a > 0 ||
  c == 0 && a == 0 && b > 0;
```

II.
```
boolean ok = a + b + c > 0 && a*b + b*c + c*a == 0;
```

III.
```
boolean ok = a > 0 || b > 0 || c > 0;
if (ok)
  ok = a + b == 0 || b + c == 0 || c + a == 0;
```

(A) I only
(B) II only
(C) I and II
(D) I and III
(E) I, II, and III

<u>Questions 12-16</u> are based on the following classes:

```
public class Person implements Comparable
{
  private String name;

  public Person(String name) { this.name = name; }
  public String getName() { return name; }

  public boolean equals(Object other)
  {
    return other != null && name.equals(((Person)other).name);
  }

  public int compareTo(Object other)
  {
    return name.compareTo(((Person)other).name);
  }

  public int hashCode() { return name.hashCode(); }
}


public class SoccerPlayer extends Person
{
  private int numGoals;

  public SoccerPlayer(String name, int n)
  {
    super(name);
    numGoals = n;
  }

  public int getNumGoals() { return numGoals; }
  public void score() { numGoals++; }

  public int compareTo(SoccerPlayer other)
  {
    return getNumGoals() - other.getNumGoals();
  }

  public String toString()
  {
    return getName() + "/" + getNumGoals();
  }
}
```

12. Which of the following declarations is invalid?

(A) `Person p = new Person("Mia Hamm");`
(B) `SoccerPlayer p = new Person("Mia Hamm");`
(C) `Comparable p = new Person("Mia Hamm");`
(D) `Person p = new SoccerPlayer("Kristine Lilly", 0);`
(E) `Comparable p = new SoccerPlayer("Kristine Lilly", 0);`

13. What is the result of the following code?

```
Person players[] =
      {new SoccerPlayer("Mia Hamm", 7),
       new SoccerPlayer("Kristine Lilly", 6)};
System.out.println(players[0].
            compareTo((SoccerPlayer)players[1])); // Line ***
```

(A) Syntax error in the class `Person`: `other.name` is not accessible
(B) Syntax error in the class `SoccerPlayer`: `compareTo` is redefined
(C) `ClassCastException` on Line ***
(D) Compiles and runs with no errors; displays 1
(E) Compiles and runs with no errors; displays 2

14.[AB] Suppose the `Person` and `SoccerPlayer` classes are changed as follows: `other.name` is replaced with `other.getName()` and `compareTo` in `SoccerPlayer` is renamed into `compareGoals`. What will be the result of the following code segment?

```
SoccerPlayer mia = new SoccerPlayer("Mia Hamm", 6);
SoccerPlayer kristine = new SoccerPlayer("Kristine Lilly", 5);
Set team = new HashSet();
team.add(mia);
team.add(kristine);
kristine.score();
team.add(kristine);
Iterator iter = team.iterator();        // Line ***
while(iter.hasNext())
  System.out.print(iter.next() + " ");
```

(A) `Kristine Lilly/5 Mia Hamm/6`
(B) `Kristine Lilly/6 Mia Hamm/6`
(C) `Mia Hamm/6 Kristine Lilly/5 Kristine Lilly/6`
(D) `Kristine Lilly/5 Kristine Lilly/6 Mia Hamm/6`
(E) Syntax error on Line ***

Questions 15-16 are concerned with a class `SoccerTeam` that represents a team of soccer players:

```
public class SoccerTeam
{
  private SoccerPlayer[] players;
  private ArrayList mvps; // holds all the players who scored
                          //   the same highest number of goals

  public void score(int k)
  {
    players[k].score();                              // Line *1*
    int goals = players[k].getNumGoals();
    int maxGoals =
      ((SoccerPlayer)mvps.get(0)).getNumGoals();     // Line *2*
    if (goals >= maxGoals)
    {
      if (goals == maxGoals)                         // Line *3*
        mvps.add(players[k]);
      else
      {
        // mvps is left with only one player in it, players[k]:
        < missing statements >
      }
    }
  }

  < constructors and other methods not shown >
}
```

15. `SoccerTeam`'s `score` method is intended to update the number of scored goals for a given player on the team and update the list of "most valuable players" (all of whom have the same score, the highest on the team). If the player's new score is higher than the old best, the `mvps` list is updated to contain only that one player. However, the `score` method has an error. Which of the following actions would correct that error?

I. Move Line *2* before Line *1*

II. Replace Line *3* with

```
if (goals == maxGoals && players[k] != mvps.get(0))
```

III. Replace Line *3* with

```
if (goals == maxGoals && !mvps.contains(players[k]))
```

(A) I only
(B) II only
(C) I and II
(D) II and III
(E) I, II, and III

16. Which of the following would be an appropriate replacement for < *missing statements* > in `SoccerTeam`'s `score` method?

(A)
```
mvps.set(0, players[k]);
```

(B)
```
mvps.resize(0);
mvps.add(players[k]);
```

(C)
```
mvps = new ArrayList();
mvps.add(players[k]);
```

(D)
```
mvps = new ArrayList(1);
mvps.set(0, players[k]);
```

(E)
```
delete mvps;
mvps = new ArrayList();
mvps.add(players[k]);
```

17.[AB] The elements in an array of size n are first increasing (`a[i] < a[i+1]`), until they reach a maximum value, then decreasing (`a[i] > a[i+1]`). What are the respective "big-O" estimates for the number of comparisons in two optimal algorithms, one that finds a maximum value in such an array and another that sorts the array in ascending order?

(A) $O(\log n)$ and $O(n)$
(B) $O(\log n)$ and $O(n \log n)$
(C) $O(n)$ and $O(n)$
(D) $O(n)$ and $O(n \log n)$
(E) $O(n)$ and $O(n^2)$

18.[AB] What is the output from the following code segment?

```
Set set = new TreeSet();
String str = "A";
set.add(str);
str += "B";
set.add(str);
str += "C";
set.add(str);
Iterator iter = set.iterator();
while (iter.hasNext())
  System.out.print(iter.next() + "-");
```

(A) `A-`
(B) `ABC-`
(C) `A-B-C-`
(D) `A-AB-ABC-`
(E) None of the above

19.[AB] Suppose `ListNode p1, p2` initially refer to two nodes in the same circular linked list. Under what condition does the following loop terminate?

```
do
{
  p1 = p1.getNext();
  p2 = p2.getNext().getNext();
} while (p1 != p2);
```

(A) Always
(B) If and only if `p1 == p2.getNext()`
(C) If and only if the total number of nodes in the list is even
(D) If and only if the number of nodes from `p2` to `p1` (excluding both ends of this segment of the list) is even
(E) If and only if the list contains two nodes with the same `info`

20.[AB] What does the following code display?

```
String expr = "(a + b) / (2 * (a - b))";
Stack stk = new ArrayStack();
int i, k;

for (k = 0; k < expr.length(); k++)
{
  if (expr.charAt(k) == '(')
  {
    stk.push(new Integer(k + 1));
  }
  else if (expr.charAt(k) == ')')
  {
    i = ((Integer)stk.pop()).intValue();
    System.out.println(expr.substring(i, k));
  }
}
```

(A)
```
(2 * (a - b))
(a - b)
(a + b)
```

(B)
```
(a - b)
(2 * (a - b))
(a + b)
```

(C)
```
a + b
a - b
2 * (a - b)
```

(D)
```
a + b
a - b
2 * a - b
```

(E)
```
a + b)
a - b)
2 * (a - b))
```

21. The following method `packed` analyzes a string passed to it and returns a new string:

```
public String packed(String msg)
{
  String packedMsg = "";

  for (int i = 0; i < msg.length(); i++)
  {
    if (msg.charAt(i) != '.')
    {
      int len = packedMsg.length();
      if (len == 0 || msg.charAt(i) != packedMsg.charAt(len-1))
        packedMsg += msg.substring(i, i+1);
    }
  }
  return packedMsg;
}
```

For which of the following values of `msg`, is `packed(msg)` NOT equal to `packed("xxo.ooo.xx.x")`?

(A) `xxo..ooo..xx..x`
(B) `..xxooooooxxxx..`
(C) `xxooooxxx`
(D) `xxooooooxxox`
(E) `xox`

22.[AB] What is the value of `sum` after the following code is executed?

```
int sum = 0;
int r = 0, c = 0;
int temp, d1 = 1, d2 = 2;
int table[][] = new int[8][8];

for (int k = 0; k < 64; k++)
{
  table[r][c] = 1;
  r = (r + d1) % 8;
  c = (c + d2) % 8;
  temp = d1; d1 = d2; d2 = temp;
}

for (r = 0; r < 8; r++)
  for (c = 0; c < 8; c++)
    sum += table[r][c];
```

(A) 8
(B) 15
(C) 16
(D) 22
(E) 64

Questions 23-24 assume that `TreeNode root` points to a root of the following binary tree:

```
      A
     / \
    B   C
   /   / \
  D   E   F
           \
            G
```

23.[AB] Consider the method `traverse`:

```
public void traverse(TreeNode root)
{
  if (root != null)
  {
    traverse(root.getLeft());
    traverse(root.getRight());
    System.out.print(root.getValue());
    traverse(root.getRight());
    traverse(root.getLeft());
  }
}
```

How many letters will be displayed when `traverse(root)` is called?

(A) 1
(B) 7
(C) 13
(D) 14
(E) 25

24.[AB] Consider the following method:

```
public void grow(TreeNode root)
{
  if (root != null)
  {
    if (root.getLeft() != null && root.getRight() == null)
      root.setRight(new TreeNode("X", null, null));
    else if (root.getLeft() == null && root.getRight() != null)
      root.setLeft(new TreeNode("X", null, null));
    grow(root.getLeft());
    grow(root.getRight());
  }
}
```

Which of the following represents the resulting tree after `grow(root)` is called?

(A)

```
      A
     / \
    /   \
   B     C
  /     / \
 D     E   F
            \
             G
              \
               X
```

(B)

```
      A
     / \
    /   \
   B     C
  / \   / \
 D   X E   F
          / \
         X   G
```

(C)

```
          A
        /   \
       /     \
      B       C
     / \     / \
    D   X   E   F
   /\   /\  /\  /\
  X  X X  X X X X  G
```

(D)

```
         A
       /   \
      /     \
     B       C
    / \     / \
   D   X   E   F
  /\       /\  /\
 X  X     X  X X  G
                 / \
                X   X
```

(E) None of the above

25. An exam contains 24 questions for 40 minutes. Some questions are easy, while other questions are really hard. Constance and Skip always solve any easy question in 20 seconds, but a hard question always takes each of them 3 minutes. Constance's strategy is to take each question in turn and take whatever time it takes to solve it. Skip tries a question for 20 seconds and if he can't solve it, he moves on to the next one. If he has looked at all the questions, Skip returns to the unsolved hard questions, but he has to start solving them from scratch because by then he's forgotten what they were about. If the first half of the test contains at least 8 easy questions and the second half contains at least 8 hard questions, which of the following statements is FALSE?

(A) Skip will solve at least 18 questions
(B) Constance will solve at least 20 questions
(C) If at most 10 of the questions are hard, both Skip and Constance will solve all 24 questions
(D) Skip will solve at most 10 hard questions
(E) Constance will always solve at least as many questions as Skip

2001

1. What is the output from the following code?

```
int a = 1, b = 2, c = 3;
a += b + c;
b += a + c;
c += a + b;
System.out.println(a + " " + b + " " + c);
```

(A) 3 3 4
(B) 3 5 6
(C) 5 4 3
(D) 5 8 13
(E) 6 11 20

2. Consider two methods:

```
public int f(int x)
{
  return x + 2;
}
```

and

```
public int g(int x)
{
  return x * 2;
}
```

What is the value of x after the following statements are executed?

```
int x = 1;
x += f(g(x)) - g(f(x));
```

(A) -9
(B) -2
(C) -1
(D) 3
(E) 7

3. What is the value of `y` after the following code is executed?

```
int x = 123, y = 0;
while (x > 0)
{
  y *= 10;
  y += x % 10;
  x /= 10;
}
```

(A) 1
(B) 3
(C) 6
(D) 12
(E) 321

4.[AB] The method `xWon` below is supposed to return `true` if a tic-tac-toe board (represented by a 3-by-3 array of characters) has three `x`'s in any line, `false` otherwise:

```
public boolean xWon (char[][] b)
{
  if (b[1][1] == 'x')
  {
    if (b[0][0] == 'x' && b[2][2] == 'x') return true;
    if (b[0][1] == 'x' && b[2][1] == 'x') return true;
    if (b[1][0] == 'x' && b[1][2] == 'x') return true;
    if (b[0][2] == 'x' && b[2][0] == 'x') return true;
  }
  else if (b[0][0] == 'x')
  {
    if (b[0][1] == 'x' && b[0][2] == 'x') return true;
    if (b[1][0] == 'x' && b[2][0] == 'x') return true;
  }
  else if (b[2][2] == 'x')
  {
    if (b[2][0] == 'x' && b[2][1] == 'x') return true;
    if (b[0][2] == 'x' && b[1][2] == 'x') return true;
  }
  return false;
}
```

However, it is coded incorrectly. For which of the following tic-tac-toe boards would `xWon` return a wrong value?

(A)	(B)	(C)	(D)	(E)
`x..`	`o.x`	`xxo`	`x.o`	`oox`
`xxo`	`ox.`	`o.o`	`oxo`	`o..`
`xoo`	`xox`	`oxx`	`x.x`	`xxx`

5. Consider the following method:

```
public void divide5(int[] a, int[] q, int[] r)
{
  q[0] = a[0] / 5;
  r[0] = a[0] % 5;
}
```

What is the value of `y[0]` after the following statements are executed?

```
int[] x = {21, 22, 23}, y = new int[3];
divide5(x, y, y);
```

(A) 0
(B) 1
(C) 2
(D) 4
(E) 21

6.[AB] Suppose the method `fun` is defined as follows:

```
public void fun(int m[][], String s)
{
  for (int i = 1; i < s.length(); i++)
  {
    int r = Character.digit(s.charAt(i), 10);
    int c = Character.digit(s.charAt(i - 1), 10);
    m[r][c]++;
  }
}
```

What is the output when the following code fragment is executed?

```
int m[][] = new int[10][10];
String s = "20012002";

fun(m, s);
int sum = 0;
for (int k = 0; k < 10; k++)
  sum += m[k][k];
System.out.println(sum);
```

(A) 1
(B) 2
(C) 4
(D) 7
(E) 8

7. Which of the following conditions is always `true` after the `while` loop in the following code fragment has finished (assuming it executes without errors)?

```
int k = 0, n = 10;
while (k < n && a[k] >= 0)
  k++;
```

(A) `k >= n && a[k] < 0`
(B) `k < n && a[k] < 0`
(C) `k < n || a[k] < 0`
(D) `k >= n || a[k] < 0`
(E) None of the above

8. The method

```
public boolean xyz(String s)
{
  return s.length() >= 3 &&
     ((s.charAt(0) == s.charAt(1) &&
           s.charAt(1) == s.charAt(2)) || xyz(s.substring(1)));
}
```

returns `true` if and only if

(A) `s` contains three or more of the same characters in a row
(B) `s` starts with three or more of the same characters
(C) `s` ends with three or more of the same characters
(D) `s` contains three or more of the same characters
(E) `s[0]` is the same as two other characters in `s`

9. The following version of Selection Sort is supposed to sort an array in ascending order. For better performance it tries to tackle the array from both ends simultaneously:

```
public void sort(int a[])
{
  int left = 0, right = a.length - 1;
  int k;

  while (left < right)
  {
    for (k = left + 1; k < right; k++)
    {
      if (a[k] < a[left])
        swap(a, k, left);
      else if (a[k] > a[right])
        swap(a, k, right);
    }
    left++;
    right--;
  }
}
```

`swap(a, i, j)` correctly swaps `a[i]` and `a[j]`. This code has a bug, though. Which of the following changes would assure that the method sorts all arrays correctly?

I. Remove `else` in

```
else if (a[k] > a[right])...
```

II. Replace

```
for (k = left + 1; k < right; k++)
```

with

```
for (k = left; k <= right; k++)
```

III. Add

```
if (a[left] > a[right])
  swap(a, left, right);
```

at the beginning of the `while` loop (before the `for` loop).

(A) I only
(B) II only
(C) III only
(D) I or II
(E) II or III

10.[AB] Insertion Sort is a sorting algorithm that works as follows: keep the first k elements of the array sorted; find the right place and insert the next element among the first k. These steps are repeated for $k = 1, ..., n$. Sequential Search is usually used to find the right spot in which to insert the next element. Suppose we use Binary Search instead of Sequential Search in this algorithm. How would big-O for the number of comparisons among the elements (not counting the number of moves or swaps) change?

(A) No change
(B) From $O(n)$ to $O(\log n)$
(C) From $O(n^2)$ to $O(n^2/2)$
(D) From $O(n^2)$ to $O(n \log n)$
(E) From $O(n^2)$ to $O(n)$

Questions 11-12 are based on the following class that represents a moving ball on a rectangular pool table:

```
public class MovingBall
{
  private int mLength, mWidth;
  private int mPosX, mPosY;
  private int mDirX, mDirY;

  public MovingBall(int length, int width, int dx, int dy)
  {
    mLength = length;
    mWidth = width;
    mPosX = length / 2;
    mPosY = width / 2;
    mDirX = dx;
    mDirY = dy;
  }

  public void move()
  {
    mPosX += mDirX;
    mPosY += mDirY;
    if (mPosX == 0 || mPosX == mLength) mDirX = -mDirX;
    if (mPosY == 0 || mPosY == mWidth) mDirY = -mDirY;
  }
}
```

11. Given

```
MovingBall b = new MovingBall(8, 4, 1, -1);
```

what are the values of `mPosX` and `mPosY` after 70 moves (i.e., 70 calls to `b.move()`)?

(A) 74 and −68
(B) 6 and 4
(C) 4 and 2
(D) 3 and 1
(E) 1 and −1

12. If

```
MovingBall b = new MovingBall(9, 4, 1, 1);
```

is defined, after how many moves (i.e., calls to `b.move()`) will ball `b` hit position `mPosX` = 6, `mPosY` = 1?

(A) Never
(B) 2
(C) 3
(D) 7
(E) 30

13. Suppose all the elements in an array have different values. Let us say the array is "nearly sorted" (in ascending order) if each element's position differs from its appropriate position in the sorted arrangement of the same array by at most 2 (in either direction). The following method takes an array where the first *n* elements are "nearly sorted" and properly sorts the array:

```
public void sortNearlySorted(int[] arr, int n)
{
  int i = 0;

  while (i < n - 1)
  {
    if (arr[i+1] < arr[i])
      swap(arr, i, i+1);
    if (i+2 < n && arr[i+2] < arr[i])
      swap(arr, i, i+2);
    i++;
  }
}
```

Which of the following is a loop invariant for the `while` loop in the above method?

(A) `arr[0] ... arr[n-1]` are sorted and `0 <= i < n`
(B) `arr[0] ... arr[n-1]` are nearly sorted and `i < n-1`
(C) `arr[0] ... arr[i-1]` are placed where they belong in the sorted array and `arr[i] ... arr[n-1]` are "nearly sorted"
(D) `arr[i] < arr[i+1]` and `arr[i] < arr[i+2]`
(E) `arr[0] ... arr[n-3]` are sorted

14. In the ABBAB language the alphabet has only two letters. A string of letters (including one-letter strings) is a valid word, if and only if the `isValid` method returns `true` for that string. `isValid` is defined as follows:

```
public boolean isValid (String word)
{
  int n = word.length();

  return n <= 1 ||
   (isValid(word.substring(0, n-1)) &&
                                word.charAt(n-1) == 'B') ||
   (isValid(word.substring(0, n-2)) &&
                                "BA".equals(word.substring(n-2)));
}
```

How many valid words of length 7 are there in the ABBAB language?

(A) 2
(B) 3
(C) 15
(D) 23
(E) 34

15.[AB] The method below takes a linked list pointed to by `head`, removes the first node, appends it at the end of the list, and returns a reference to the head of the new list.

```
public ListNode firstToLast(ListNode head)
{
  if (head == null || head.getNext() == null)
    return head;

  ListNode p = head;
  while (p.getNext() != null)
    p = p.getNext();

  < missing statements >

  return head;
}
```

Which of the following code fragments correctly completes this method?

I.
```
ListNode temp = head;
head = head.getNext();
p.setNext(temp);
temp.setNext(null);
```

II.
```
ListNode temp = head.getNext();
head.setNext(null);
p.setNext(head);
head = temp;
```

III.
```
p.setNext(head);
head = head.getNext();
p.getNext().setNext(null);
```

(A) I only
(B) II only
(C) I and II
(D) II and III
(E) I, II, and III

16.[AB] The following method `goodHand` checks whether a stack of `Integers` (that represent ranks of playing cards in a small deck) has a certain property:

```
public boolean goodHand(Stack hand)
{
  int[] count = new int[2];
  Object x, y;

  for (int k = 0; k <= 1; k++)
  {
    if (hand.isEmpty())
      return false;
    x = hand.pop();
    Stack stk = new ArrayStack();
    while (!hand.isEmpty())
    {
      y = hand.pop();
      if (x.equals(y))
        count[k]++;
      else
        stk.push(y);
    }
    hand = stk;
  }
  return Math.abs(count[0] - count[1]) <= 1 && hand.isEmpty();
}
```

For which of the following stacks does `goodHand` return `true`?

	(A)	(B)	(C)	(D)	(E)
top ==>	2	2	2	3	2
	3	2	3	3	2
	4	3	2	3	2
	5	3	2	3	2
	6	4	3	2	2

17.[AB] An n by n square image contains white and black pixels. The first several columns contain one or more black pixels at the top with only white pixels below; the remaining columns are all white. For example:

```
xxxx..
xxxx..
x.x[x]..
x.x...
..x...
......
```

A program is allowed to examine individual pixels in the image; its task is to find the position of the lowest black pixel in the rightmost column that has at least one black pixel (the boxed pixel in the above example). What is the worst-case big-O for the number of examined pixels in the best possible algorithm?

(A) $O(\log n)$
(B) $O((\log n)^2)$
(C) $O(n)$
(D) $O(n \log n)$
(E) $O(n^2)$

Questions 18-22 use the following classes:

```
public class Point
{
  private int x;
  private int y;

  public Point(int x, int y) { this.x = x; this.y = y; }

  public int getX() { return x; }
  public int getY() { return y; }

  public boolean equals(Point other)
  {
    return getX() == other.getX() && getY() == other.getY();
  }

  public int hashCode()
  {
    return (new Integer(getX() + getY())).hashCode();
  }

  public void setX(int x) { this.x = x; }
  public void setY(int y) { this.y = y; }

  public String toString()
  {
    return "(" + getX() + ", " + getY() + ")";
  }
}


public class MovingPoint extends Point
{
  private Point myPoint;

  public MovingPoint(Point p)
  {
    < missing statements >
    myPoint = p;
  }

  public int getX() { return myPoint.getX(); }
  public int getY() { return myPoint.getY(); }

  public void move(int x, int y)
  {
    myPoint.setX(x);
    myPoint.setY(y);
  }

  public String toString()
  {
    return myPoint.toString();
  }
}
```

18. Which of the following can replace < *missing statements* > in `MovingPoint`'s constructor?

(A) `super();`
(B) `super(0, 0);`
(C) `setX(0); setY(0);`
(D) `super(); setX(p.getX()); setY(p.getY());`
(E) `// set myPoint to p:`

19. Which line in the following code segment causes a syntax error?

```
Point p1 = new Point(100, 100);         // Line 1
MovingPoint p2 = new MovingPoint(p1); // Line 2
Point p3 = new MovingPoint(p2);         // Line 3
MovingPoint p4 = new MovingPoint(p2); // Line 4
```

(A) No syntax errors in these lines
(B) Line 1
(C) Line 2
(D) Line 3
(E) Line 4

20. What is the output of the following code?

```
Point p = new Point(0, 0);
MovingPoint mp = new MovingPoint(p);
mp.move(1, 1);
System.out.println(p + " " + p.equals(mp));
```

(A) `NullPointerException`
(B) `ClassCastException`
(C) `(0, 0) true`
(D) `(0, 0) false`
(E) `(1, 1) true`

21.[AB] Consider the following two code segments:

```
Set points = new HashSet();
MovingPoint p;

p = new MovingPoint(
        new Point(0, 0));
points.add(p);

p = new MovingPoint(
        new Point(0, 2));
points.add(p);

p = new MovingPoint(
        new Point(2, 2));
points.add(p);

p = new MovingPoint(
        new Point(2, 0));
points.add(p);

p = new MovingPoint(
        new Point(1, 1));
points.add(p);

System.out.print(points.size());
```

```
Set points = new HashSet();
MovingPoint p;

p = new MovingPoint(
        new Point(0, 0));
points.add(p);

p.move(0, 2);

points.add(p);

p.move(2, 2);

points.add(p);

p.move(2, 0);

points.add(p);

p.move(1, 1);

points.add(p);

System.out.print(points.size());
```

What are their respective outputs?

(A) 3 and 1
(B) 3 and 3
(C) 5 and 1
(D) 5 and 3
(E) 5 and 5

22.[AB] What is the output of the following code segment?

```
Point p = new Point(0, 0);
MovingPoint p1 = new MovingPoint(p);
MovingPoint p2 = new MovingPoint(p);
Queue q = new ListQueue();
p1.move(1, 0);
q.enqueue(p1);
p2.move(0, 1);
q.enqueue(p2);
System.out.println(q.dequeue() + " " + q.dequeue());
```

(A) (0, 0) (0, 0)
(B) (1, 0) (1, 0)
(C) (0, 1) (0, 1)
(D) (1, 0) (0, 1)
(E) (0, 1) (1, 0)

23.[AB] Consider the following method:

```
public int magic(TreeNode root)
{
  if (root != null)
  {
    if (root.getLeft() == null && root.getRight() == null)
      return 0;
    if (magic(root.getLeft()) + magic(root.getRight()) == 0)
    {
      TreeNode temp = root.getLeft();
      root.setLeft(root.getRight());
      root.setRight(temp);
    }
  }
  return -1;
}
```

What does this method do to a tree referred to by `root`?

(A) Nothing, leaves the tree unchanged
(B) Swaps the left and right branches of the tree at the root
(C) Replaces the tree with its mirror image
(D) Swaps any two leaves that have the same parent
(E) Swaps the leftmost and the rightmost leaves

24.[AB] Suppose `traversePreOrder` and `traversePostOrder` are defined as follows:

```
public void traversePreOrder(TreeNode root, Stack s)
{
  if (root != null)
  {
    s.push(root.getValue());
    traversePreOrder(root.getLeft(), s);
    traversePreOrder(root.getRight(), s);
  }
}

public void traversePostOrder(TreeNode root, Stack s)
{
  if (root != null)
  {
    traversePostOrder(root.getLeft(), s);
    traversePostOrder(root.getRight(), s);
    root.setValue(s.pop());
  }
}
```

If `root` initially refers to

```
      A
     / \
    /   \
   B     C
  / \   / \
 D   E F   G
```

what is the resulting tree after the following statements are executed?

```
Stack s = new ArrayStack();
traversePreOrder(root, s);
traversePostOrder(root, s);
```

(A)

```
      A
     / \
    /   \
   B     C
  / \   / \
 D   E F   G
```

(B)

```
      A
     / \
    /   \
   C     B
  / \   / \
 G   F E   D
```

(C)

```
      G
     / \
    /   \
   D     F
  / \   / \
 A   B E   C
```

(D)

```
      A
     / \
    /   \
   C     B
  / \   / \
 F   G D   E
```

(E)

```
      G
     / \
    /   \
   F     D
  / \   / \
 E   C B   A
```

25. A multiple-choice question offers three options, I, II, and III, and asks which ones fit into a given situation. The offered answers are a) I only; b) II only; c) III only; d) I and II; and e) II and III. Assuming that it takes the same amount of time to examine any one of the three options, that the odds that any option fits are 50-50, and that a student always gets all answers right and doesn't waste time considering unnecessary options, which option should she consider first?

(A) Doesn't matter
(B) Either I or II
(C) Either I or III
(D) Definitely I
(E) Definitely II

2000

1. Which of the following statements does NOT display `2/3`?

(A) `System.out.println("2/3");`
(B) `System.out.println("2" + "/" + "3");`
(C) `System.out.println(2/3);`
(D) `System.out.println(2 + "/" + 3);`
(E) `System.out.println((int)2 + "/" + (int)3);`

2. If array `arr` has five elements with values `0 1 2 3 4`, what are the values in `arr` after the following code is executed?

```
for (int k = 0; k < 5; k++)
  arr[k] = arr[arr[k]];
```

(A) `0 1 2 3 4`
(B) `1 2 3 4 0`
(C) `1 2 2 2 2`
(D) `0 0 0 0 0`
(E) `1 2 3 4 4`

3. If `c` and `d` are `boolean` variables, which one of the answer choices is NOT equivalent to the following expression?

```
(c && d) != (c || d)
```

(A) `(c && !d) || (!c && d)`
(B) `(c || d) && (!c && !d)`
(C) `(c || d) && (!c || !d)`
(D) `(c || d) && !(c && d)`
(E) `c != d`

4. The value of $\left(1+\frac{1}{n}\right)^n$ for a large enough n (e.g., $n \geq 50$) approximates the base of the natural logarithm $e = 2.71828...$ A student decided to test this property and wrote the following method:

```
public double approxE()
{
  double e = 1.0 + 1.0 / 64;
  for (int count = 1; count <= 6; count++)
    e *= e;
  return e;
}
```

What value is returned by `approxE()`?

(A) No value is returned: the method throws an `ArithmeticException`
(B) 1.0
(C) 2.6973449525651
(D) 1.642359568597906
(E) 7.275669793128421

5. What is the output from the following code?

```
int[] counts = new int[3];
int i, j;
for (i = 0; i < 100; i++)
  for (j = 0; j < 10; j++)
    counts[j % 3]++;
System.out.println((counts[1] + counts[2]) / counts[0]);
```

(A) `1`
(B) `1.5`
(C) `2`
(D) `2.5`
(E) `3`

6. Suppose an array A has n elements. Let's call it periodic with a period of p if $0 < p < n$ and $A[i] == A[i+p]$ for all $0 \le i < n-p$ and p is the smallest such number. What is the period of array `v` after the following code is executed?

```
int v[] = new int[100];
v[0] = 0; v[1] = 1;

for (int i = 2; i < 100; i++)
  v[i] = v[i-1] - v[i-2];
```

(A) 2
(B) 3
(C) 4
(D) 6
(E) No period

7. What is the output from the following code?

```
StringBuffer s = new StringBuffer("WYOMING");
int k, i, n = s.length();
char temp;

for (k = 0; k < 3; k++)
{
  temp = s.charAt(n-1);
  for (i = k+1; i < n; i++)
    s.setCharAt(i, s.charAt(i-1));
  s.setCharAt(k, temp);
}
System.out.println(s);
```

(A) `YOMINGW`
(B) `MINGWYO`
(C) `GWWWWWW`
(D) `MINGOYW`
(E) `GNIMOYW`

8. A recursive method `upNdown` is defined as follows:

```
public void upNdown(int n)
{
  if (n > 1)
  {
    if (n % 2 != 0) upNdown(n+1);
    else upNdown(n/2);
    System.out.print("*");
  }
}
```

How many stars are displayed when `upNdown(5)` is called?

(A) 1
(B) 2
(C) 3
(D) 4
(E) 5

9. Given

```
String a = "a", b = "b", zero = "";
Integer c = new Integer(0);
```

what is the output of

```
System.out.println(
  ((a+b)+c).equals(a+(b+c)) + " " +
  (c + zero).equals(zero + c) + " " +
  (a + null).equals(a + "null"));
```

(A) `false false false`
(B) `false true true`
(C) `true false true`
(D) `true true false`
(E) `true true true`

10.[AB] The method below uses a stack to check whether parentheses and brackets match in a string of characters:

```
public boolean parensAndBracketsMatch(String expr)
{
  Stack s = new ArrayStack();
  char ch0, ch;

  for (int k = 0; k < expr.length(); k++)
  {
    ch = expr.charAt(k);
    if (ch == '(' || ch == '[')
      s.push(new Character(ch));
    else if (ch == ')' || ch == ']')
    {
      if (s.isEmpty())
        return false;
      ch0 = ((Character)s.pop()).charValue();
      if ((ch0 == '(' && ch != ')') ||
        (ch0 == '[' && ch != ']'))
         return false;
    }
  }
  return true;
}
```

However, it has a bug. For which of the following strings does this method return a result that is DIFFERENT from what is expected?

		<u>*Expected result:*</u>
(A)	`"[(a+b)*(c+d)]/2"`	`true`
(B)	`"[(a+b)*(c+d)/2]"`	`true`
(C)	`"[(a+b)*(c+d)]/2["`	`false`
(D)	`"](a+b)*(c+d)/2["`	`false`
(E)	`"[(a+b]*[c+d)/2]"`	`false`

11. Consider the following two versions of the method `mixUp`:

```
public void mixUp(int[] x,
                  int[] y)
{
  x[0] = x[0] - 2 * x[0] * y[1];
  y[1] = y[1] - 2 * x[0] * y[0];
}
```

```
public void mixUp(int[] x,
                  int[] y)
{
  int d = 2 * x[0] * y[1];
  x[0] -= d;
  y[1] -= d;
}
```

Suppose the following arrays are declared and initialized:

```
int[] a = {1, 1}, b = {0, 0}, c = {1, 1};
```

Which of the following calls to `mixUp` result in the same values in `a`, `b`, and `c` for both versions of the code?

I. `mixUp(a, a)`
II. `mixUp(a, b)`
III. `mixUp(a, c)`

(A) I only
(B) II only
(C) I and II
(D) II and III
(E) I, II, and III

12. The Binary Search algorithm normally finds a value in an array sorted in ascending order. Suppose that by mistake the algorithm is used on an unsorted array with the following seven elements:

```
1 3 2 5 13 8 21
```

Which of the following target values will NOT be found?

(A) `1`
(B) `3`
(C) `5`
(D) `13`
(E) `21`

13. An array has $4095 = 2^{12} - 1$ elements, arranged in ascending order. Binary Search is used to find the position of a target value. This Binary Search is implemented iteratively, in such a way that in each iteration the `target` is compared to one of the elements of the array. Suppose we know that the `target` is somewhere in the array. What number of iterations guarantees that a target value is found?

(A) 10
(B) 11
(C) 12
(D) 2047
(E) 4095

14. Which of the following arithmetic expressions maps the values $x = 0, 1, 2, 3, 4, 5, 6$ onto $y = 4, 3, 9, 8, 7, 6, 5$, respectively?

(A) `y = 11 - x + (x + 4) % 7;`
(B) `y = (4 - x) % 7 + 2 * x;`
(C) `y = 3 + (8 - x) % 7;`
(D) `y = 9 - (x - 2) % 7;`
(E) `y = 4 + x % 7 - 2 * x;`

15.[AB] The method below implements a simplified square cipher:

```
public char[][] encrypt(char[][] key, String msg)
{
  int i, j, n = key.length, k = 0;
  char[][] result = new char[n][n];  // fills with spaces

  for (i = 0; i < n; i++)
    for (j = 0; j < n; j++)
      if (key[i][j] == 'x')
        result[i][j] = msg.charAt(k++);

  for (i = 0; i < n; i++)
    for (j = 0; j < n; j++)
      if (key[i][j] == 'x')
        result[n-i-1][n-j-1] = msg.charAt(k++);

  return result;
}
```

If `key` is a 4 by 4 matrix

```
.x..
x..x
.xx.
xx.x
```

and `msg` is `"ransom received "`, which of the following matrices is returned from `encrypt(key, msg)`?

(A)
```
rean
csoe
mivr
d e
```

(B)
```
 rde
avin
esoc
m er
```

(C)
```
 rvc
aein
dsoe
m er
```

(D)
```
rdsr
 no
aeve
iemc
```

(E)
```
rcan
esoi
mvre
d ee
```

Questions 16-17 use the following class:

```
public class Circle
{
  private int xCenter, yCenter, radius;

  public  Circle(int x, int y, int r)
  {
    xCenter = x;
    yCenter = y;
    radius = r;
  }

  public void moveTo(int x, int y)
  {
    xCenter = x;
    yCenter = y;
  }

  // Draw this circle in the graphics context g
  public void draw(Graphics g) { < code not shown > }
}
```

16. Suppose the following code is added to a method that repaints a window within a graphics context g:

```
for (int x = 10; x <= 30; x += 10)
{
  Circle circle = new Circle(x + 100, 100, x);
  circle.draw(g);
}
```

The origin of the coordinate system is in the upper left corner of the window with the *y*-axis pointing down. Which of the following pictures will be displayed?

(A)

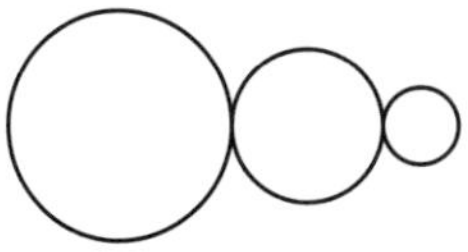

(B)

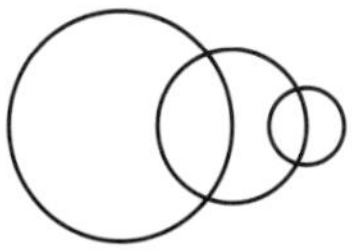

(C)

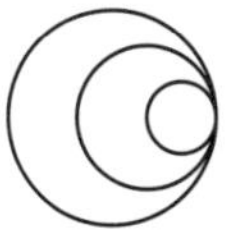

(D)

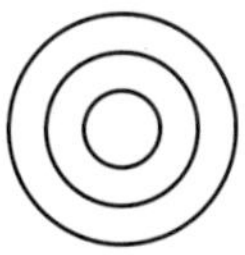

(E)

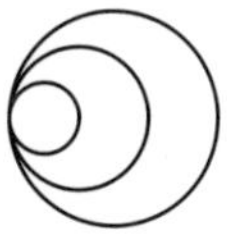

17. The method `drawOrnament` draws several circles, as follows:

```
public void drawOrnament(Graphics g, int k)
{
  if (k < 8)
    return;
  Circle c = new Circle(100 - k, 100 - k, k);
  c.draw(g);
  c.moveTo(100 + k, 100 + k);
  c.draw(g);
  drawOrnament(g, k/2);
}
```

Which of the following pictures is produced by `drawOrnament(g, 32)`?

(A)

(B)

(C)

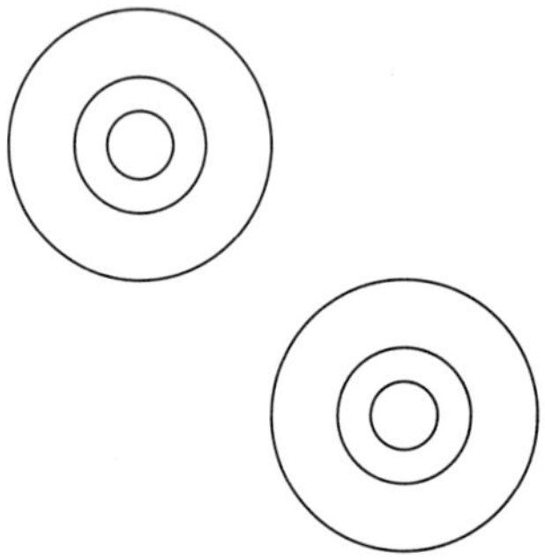

(D)

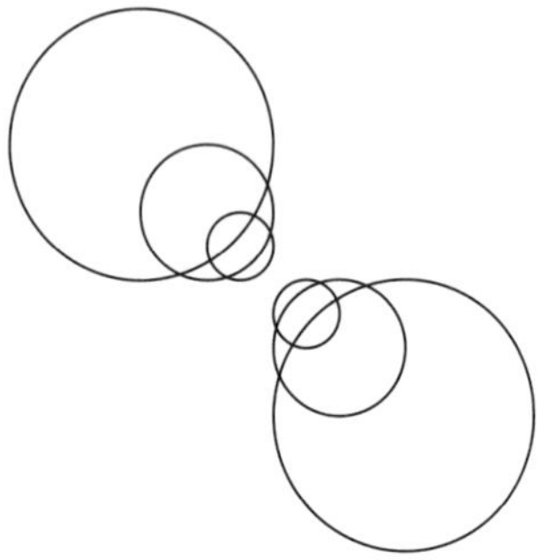

(E)

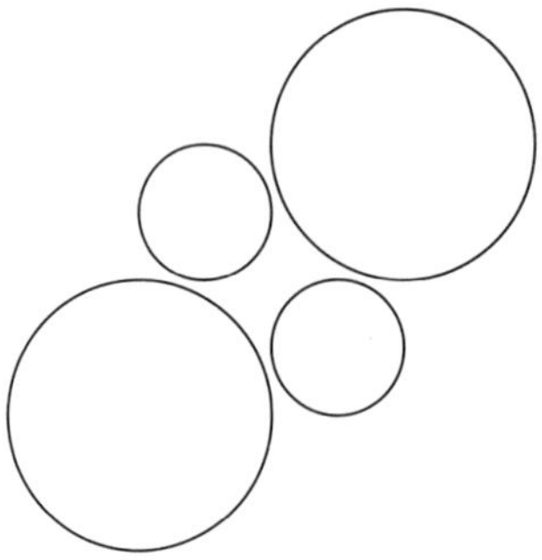

18. What is displayed by

```
System.out.println(expand(expand("1001")));
```

where `expand` is defined as follows?

```
public String expand(String s)
{
  String d = "";

  for (int i = 0; i < s.length(); i++)
    switch (s.charAt(i))
    {
      case '0': d += "01"; break;
      case '1': d += "10"; break;
      default: d += "*"; break;
    }
  return d;
}
```

(A) `1001`
(B) `1*0*0*1*`
(C) `10010110`
(D) `10*01*01*10*`
(E) `1001011001101001`

Questions 19-21 use the following interface and class:

```
public interface Toggleable
{
  void toggle();
  boolean isOn();
}


public class ToggleSwitch implements Toggleable
{
  private boolean on;

  public ToggleSwitch() { on = false; }
  public ToggleSwitch(boolean state) { on = state; }

  public void toggle() { on = !on; }
  public boolean isOn() { return on; }
}
```

19. Suppose we have found the `ToggleSwitch.class` file but have no access to its source code. Which of the following code segments, if compiles with no errors, will convince us that `ToggleSwitch` implements `Toggleable`?

I.
```
Toggleable x = new ToggleSwitch();
```

II.
```
ToggleSwitch x = new ToggleSwitch();
x.toggle();
```

III.
```
ToggleSwitch x = new ToggleSwitch();
if (!x.isOn()) x.toggle();
```

(A) I only
(B) II only
(C) III only
(D) II and III
(E) I, II, and III

20. Consider the following class that represents a set of checkboxes:

```
public class CheckBoxSet
{
  private Toggleable[] buttons;

  public CheckBoxSet(int nButtons)
  {
    < missing statements >
  }

  public int numButtons() { return buttons.length; }
  public void push(int k) { buttons[k].toggle(); }
  public boolean isOn(int k) { return buttons[k].isOn(); }

  public void clear()
  {
    for (int k = 0; k < buttons.length; k++)
      if (buttons[k].isOn())
        buttons[k].toggle();
  }
}
```

Which of the following can replace < *missing statements* > in the `CheckBoxSet` constructor?

I.
```
buttons = new Toggleable[nButtons];
for (int k = 0; k < buttons.length; k++)
  buttons[k] = new ToggleSwitch();
```

II.
```
buttons = new ToggleSwitch[nButtons];
clear();
```

III.
```
buttons = new ToggleSwitch[nButtons];
for (int i = 0; i < buttons.length; i++)
  if (buttons[i].isOn())
    buttons[i].toggle();
```

(A) I only
(B) II only
(C) I and II
(D) II and III
(E) I, II, and III

21.[AB] A set of "radio buttons" is a user interface control used to choose one of several options. For example:

○ small ○ medium ◉ large

Consider the following class `RadioSet` that implements a set of radio buttons:

```
public class RadioSet extends CheckBoxSet
{
  // precondition:  nButtons > k >= 0
  // postcondition: creates an array of nButtons buttons and
  //                sets the k-th button to "on"
  public RadioSet(int nButtons, int k)
  {
    super(nButtons);
    push(k);
  }

  // postcondition: sets the k-th button to "on," all other
  //                buttons to "off"
  public void push(int k)
  {
    < missing code >
  }

  // postcondition: returns the number of the button that is "on";
  //                throws an exception if none are "on"
  {
    for (int k = 0; k < numButtons(); k++)
      if (isOn(k))
        return k;
    throw new IllegalStateException();
  }
}
```

Which of the following can replace < *missing code* > in this class?

I.
```
clear()
push(k);
```

II.
```
clear()
super.push(k);
```

III.
```
for (int j = 0; j < numButtons(); j++)
  if (buttons[j].isOn())
    buttons[j].toggle();
buttons[k].toggle();
```

(A) I only
(B) II only
(C) I and II
(D) II and III
(E) I, II, and III

22.[AB] `char[][] m` holds the following picture:

```
........
..xxxxx.
..xx....
..xxx...
....xxx.
......x.
.x.xxx..
..xxx...
........
```

What picture is stored in `m` after `process(m)` is called? The method `process` is defined as follows:

```
public void process(char[][] m)
{
  int rows = m.length, cols = m[0].length, r, c;
  char[][] t = new char[rows][cols];

  for (r = 0; r < rows; r++)
    for (c = 0; c < cols; c++)
      t[r][c] = m[r][c];

  for (r = 1; r < rows; r++)
    for (c = 1; c < cols; c++)
      if (t[r][c] == 'x' && (t[r-1][c] != 'x'
                            || t[r][c-1] != 'x'))
        m[r][c] = 'x';
      else
        m[r][c] = '.';
}
```

(A)	(B)	(C)	(D)	(E)
`........`	`........`	`........`	`........`	`........`
`..xxxxxx`	`..xxxxx.`	`..xxxxx.`	`...xxxx.`	`..xxxxx.`
`..xxxxx.`	`..x.....`	`........`	`...x....`	`..xxx...`
`..xxxx..`	`..x.x...`	`..xxx...`	`...xx...`	`..xxx...`
`..xxxxxx`	`....xxx.`	`.....xx.`	`.....xx.`	`....xxx.`
`....xxxx`	`......x.`	`........`	`........`	`......x.`
`.xxxxxx.`	`.x.xxx..`	`.x.xxx..`	`....xx..`	`.x.xxxx.`
`.xxxxx..`	`..x.....`	`..x.....`	`...xx...`	`..xxxx..`
`..x.....`	`........`	`........`	`........`	`........`

23. Suppose Mergesort is implemented as follows:

```
public void sort(int[] a, int n1, int n2)
{
  if (n1 == n2)
    return;
  else if (n2 == n1 + 1)
  {
    if (a[n2] < a[n1])
      swap(a, n1, n2);     // swaps a[n1] and a[n2]
    return;
  }
  int m = (n1 + n2) / 2;
  sort(a, n1, m);
  sort(a, m+1, n2);
  if (a[m] > a[m+1])
    merge (a, n1, m, n2); // merges a[n1]...a[m] and a[m+1]...a[n2]
}
```

How many times will the method `merge` be called if an array `a` contains the values

```
2 1 4 3 6 5 8 7
```

and `sort(a,0,7)` is called?

(A) 7
(B) 4
(C) 3
(D) 1
(E) 0

24.[AB] Consider the following method:

```
public void xQ(Queue q)
{
  if (q.isEmpty())
    return;

  Queue q1 = new ListQueue(), q2 = new ListQueue();
  Object x = q.dequeue();

  while (!q.isEmpty())
  {
    Object y = q.dequeue();
    if (((Comparable)y).compareTo(x) <= 0)
      q1.enqueue(y);
    else
      q2.enqueue(y);
  }

  xQ(q1);
  xQ(q2);

  while (!q1.isEmpty())
    q.enqueue(q1.dequeue());

  q.enqueue(x);

  while (!q2.isEmpty())
    q.enqueue(q2.dequeue());
}
```

What are the values in `q` after `xQ(q)` is called, if `q` initially holds `Integer` objects with the values `7,11,3,5,6,0` (listed starting from the front)?

(A) `0,3,5,6,7,11`
(B) `0,6,5,3,11,7`
(C) `3,5,6,0,7,11`
(D) `11,3,5,6,0,7`
(E) `11,7,6,5,3,0`

25.[AB] Consider the following method:

```
public int xSum(TreeNode root)
{
  if (root == null)
    return 0;
  else
    return ((Integer)root.getValue()).intValue() +
         xSum(root.getRight()) - xSum(root.getLeft());
}
```

What value is returned by `xSum(root)` if `root` points to the following tree?

```
        5
       / \
      4   2
     /   / \
    3   7   1
             \
              12
```

(A) -9
(B) -10
(C) 5
(D) 12
(E) 20

1999

1. What is the output from the following code?

```
int x = 5, y = 2;
System.out.println(x/y - (double)(x/y));
```

(A) `0`
(B) `0.5`
(C) `-0.5`
(D) `-2.5`
(E) None of the above

2. What are the values of `u` and `v` after the following code is executed?

```
int u = 3, v = 5;

u += v;
v += u;
u -= v;
v -= u;
```

(A) `0, 0`
(B) `3, 5`
(C) `5, 3`
(D) `-5, -3`
(E) `-5, 18`

3. Which of the following statements DOES NOT display `9.95`?

(A) `System.out.println(9 + 0.95);`
(B) `System.out.println(995/100.0);`
(C) `System.out.println(9. + 95/100);`
(D) `System.out.println(9 + 95.0/100);`
(E) `System.out.println(9 + "." + 95);`

4. What is the output from the following code?

```
int count1 = 0, count2 = 0, inc = 1;
for (int i = 0; i < 11; i++)
{
  count1 += inc;
  inc = -inc;
  count2 += inc;
}
System.out.println(count1 - count2);
```

(A) `0`
(B) `2`
(C) `-2`
(D) `22`
(E) `-22`

5. What is the result of the following code segment?

```
Integer i = new Integer(0);                                   // Line 1
if (!i.equals(0))                                             // Line 2
  System.out.println(i + " is not equal to " + 0); // Line 3
else
  System.out.println("Done");
```

(A) Syntax error on Line 2
(B) Syntax error on Line 3
(C) `ClassCastException`
(D) `0 is not equal to 0`
(E) `Done`

6. What is the output from the following code?

```
int a = 0, b = 0;
while (a < 3)
{
  switch (a + b)
  {
    case 0: a++;
    case 1:
    case 2: b++; break;
    case 3: a++; break;
    default: b = 0; break;
  }
  System.out.print(b);
}
```

(A) `0123`
(B) `122011`
(C) `0122011`
(D) `0122123`
(E) `112300`

7. What is the value of n after the following code is executed?

```
int i, n = 0;
while (n < 90)
{
  for (i = 0; i < 10; i++)
  {
    n += 3;
    if (n > 50)
      break;
  }
  n++;
}
```

(A) 51
(B) 61
(C) 91
(D) 93
(E) 104

8. What is the set of all possible outputs of the following code when the user correctly follows the input instructions and the program terminates without an error?

```
System.out.print(
    "Enter an integer from -1000 to 1000 (inclusive): ");

int n = console.readInt();    // Read an integer

while (n > 0 && Math.sqrt(n) < 10.0)
  n++;

System.out.println(n);
```

(A) {0, ..., 99, 100}
(B) {100, ..., 999, 1000}
(C) {-1000, -999, ..., 0} ∪ {100, ..., 999, 1000}
(D) {-1000, -999, ..., 0, ..., 999, 1000}
(E) {-1000, -999, ..., 0, ..., 99}

9. An integer array a has 19 elements. What is the value of the middle element after the following code is executed?

```
int i, j, n = 19;

for (i = 0; i < n; i++)
  a[i] = i+1;

for (i = 0, j = n-1; i <= j; i++, j--)
  a[(i+j)/2] -= (a[i] + a[j]) / 2;
```

(A) 0
(B) 10
(C) -41
(D) -62
(E) -71

10. Consider the following method:

```
public void mysteryMix(Integer a, Integer b)
{
  a = new Integer(2 * a.intValue());
  b = a;
}
```

What is the output of the following code?

```
Integer a = new Integer(1);
Integer b = new Integer(2);
mysteryMix(a, a);
mysteryMix(a, b);
System.out.println(a + " " + b);
```

(A) 1 1
(B) 1 2
(C) 2 2
(D) 1 4
(E) 4 4

11. The following interface `Index` describes the location of a document:

```
public interface Index
{
  String getKey();
  Document getAddress();
}
```

`Document` is a class that has a public method `getSize()`. An `ArrayList folder` contains `Index` objects and describes a collection of documents. Which of the following expressions refers to `size` of the *k*-th document in `folder`?

(A) `folder[k-1].getAddress().getSize()`
(B) `(Index)folder.get(k-1).getAddress().getSize()`
(C) `((Index)folder.get(k-1)).getAddress().getSize()`
(D) `((Document)(folder[k-1].getAddress())).getSize()`
(E) `((Document)(folder.get(k-1).getAddress())).getSize()`

12. Which of the following could safely appear and make sense in place of < *condition* > in some suitable context?

```
if ( < condition > )
  msg = new Message("o");
```

I. `msg == null || msg.getStatus().equals("x")`

II. `msg.getStatus().equals("x") || msg == null`

III. `"x".equals(msg.getStatus()) || msg == null`

(A) I only
(B) II only
(C) I and II
(D) II and III
(E) I, II, and III

Questions 13-17 refer to the following interface and classes used in a picture drawing application:

```
public interface Drawable
{
  void draw(Graphics g);
}


public class Line implements Drawable
{
  private int xBeg, yBeg, xEnd, yEnd;

  public Line(int x0, int y0, int x1, int y1)
  {
    xBeg = x0; yBeg = y0; xEnd = x1; yEnd = y1;
  }

  public void draw(Graphics g)
  {
    g.drawLine(xBeg, yBeg, xEnd, yEnd);
  }
}


public class Picture implements Drawable
{
  private List pictures;

  public Picture()
  {
    pictures = new LinkedList();
  }

  public void add(Drawable obj)
  {
    pictures.add(obj);
  }

  public void draw(Graphics g)
  {
    Iterator it = pictures.iterator();
    while (it.hasNext())
      ((Drawable)it.next()).draw(g);
  }
}
```

13. Which of the following code segments compiles with no errors?

(A)
```
Drawable picture = new Picture(new Line(0, 0, 100, 100));
```

(B)
```
Drawable picture = new Picture();
picture.add(new Line(0, 0, 100, 100));
```

(C)
```
Picture picture1 = new Picture();
Picture picture2 = new Picture(picture1);
```

(D)
```
Picture picture = new Picture();
picture.pictures.add(new Line(0, 0, 100, 100));
```

(E)
```
Drawable picture = new Picture();
((Picture)picture).add(new Picture());
```

14. Consider the following code segment:

```
Picture picture = new Picture();
picture.add(new Line(100, 100, 200, 50));
picture.add(new Line(200, 50, 300, 100));
Picture box = new Picture();
picture.add(box);
box.add(new Line(100, 100, 100, 300));
box.add(new Line(100, 300, 300, 300));
box.add(new Line(300, 300, 300, 100));
box.add(new Line(300, 100, 100, 100));
```

Which of the following pictures will be displayed when `picture.draw(g)` is called from an appropriate `paint` method within the graphics context `g`?

(A)

Empty picture

(B)

(C)

(D)

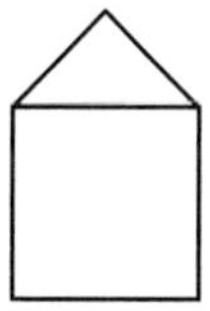

(E)

15. Suppose the class `Box` extends `Picture` and has the following constructor:

```
public Box(int x, int y, int width, int height)
{
  super();
  add(new Line(x, y, x + width, y));
  add(new Line(x + width, y, x + width, y + height));
  add(new Line(x + width, y + height, x, y + height));
  add(new Line(x, y + height, x, y));
}
```

Suppose the statements

```
Box box = new Box(100, 100, 300, 200);
box.draw(g);
```

— when executed from an appropriate `paint` method within the graphics context `g` — draw a box with the upper left corner at (100, 100), width 300 and height 200. Besides the above constructor, which methods must be supplied in the `Box` class for this to happen?

(A) No methods are needed
(B) `add(Drawable)`
(C) `draw(Graphics)`
(D) `add(Drawable)` and `draw(Graphics)`
(E) `add(Drawable)`, `add(Line)`, and `draw(Graphics)`

16. Suppose the following methods have been added to the `Line` class:

```
public String getName() { return "Line"; }

public String toString()
{
  return "[" + getName() +
       /*   " " + xBeg + " " + yBeg +
            " " + + xEnd + " " + yEnd +   */
       "]";
}
```

Also, the following methods have been added to the `Picture` class:

```
public String getName() { return "Picture"; }

public String toString()
{
  String str = "[" + getName() + " ";
  Iterator it = pictures.iterator();
  while (it.hasNext())
    str += it.next();
  return  str + "]";
}
```

Finally, the following method has been added to the `Box` class mentioned in the previous question:

```
public String getName() { return "Box"; }
```

What is the output of the following code?

```
Box box = new Box(100, 100, 100, 100);
box.add(new Line(100, 100, 200, 200));
box.add(new Line(100, 200, 200, 100));
Picture picture = new Picture();
picture.add(box);
System.out.println(picture);
```

(A) `[Picture [Line][Line][Line][Line]][Line][Line]`
(B) `[Picture [Box [Line][Line][Line][Line]]]`
(C) `[Picture [Box [Line][Line][Line][Line][Line][Line]]]`
(D) `[Picture [Picture [Line][Line][Line][Line]][Line][Line]]`
(E) `[Picture [Picture [Line][Line][Line][Line][Line][Line]]]`

17. The class `DrawingBoard` extends `JFrame` and represents a window on the screen:

```
public class DrawingBoard extends javax.swing.JFrame
{
  private Drawable picture;

  public DrawingBoard(Drawable picture)
  { this.picture = picture; }

  public void paint(Graphics g) { picture.draw(g); }
}
```

Consider the following code segment:

```
  Picture picture = new Picture();
  picture.add(picture);                         // Line ***
  DrawingBoard w = new DrawingBoard(picture);
  w.setBounds(50, 50, 400, 400);
  w.show();
```

What happens when we try to compile and execute this code?

(A) Syntax error on Line ***
(B) `ClassCastException`
(C) The code compiles and runs, but goes into an infinite loop
(D) `StackOverflowError`
(E) The code compiles and runs; a blank window is displayed

Questions 18-19 use the following class:

```
public class PetDog implements Comparable
{
  private String myName, myBreed;

  public PetDog (String name, String breed)
  { myName = name; myBreed = breed; }

  public String getName() { return myName; }
  public String getBreed() { return myBreed; }

  public boolean equals(Object other)
  { return other != null && getName().equals(other.toString()); }

  public int compareTo(Object other)
  {
    return getName().compareTo(other.toString());
  }

  public int hashCode() { return getName().hashCode(); }

  public String toString()
  { return getName() + " -- " + getBreed(); }
}
```

Suppose the following variables are declared and initialized:

```
PetDog honey = new PetDog("Honey", "Cocker Spaniel");
PetDog lucie = new PetDog("Lucie", "Springer Spaniel");
PetDog murray = new PetDog("Murray", "Golden Retriever");
```

18.[AB] The following code segment should display

```
Honey is a Cocker Spaniel
```

```
Map map = new HashMap();
map.put(honey.getName(), honey);
map.put(lucie.getName(), lucie);
map.put(murray.getName(), murray);

System.out.println(honey.getName() + " is a " +
                                  < missing expression > );
```

Which of the following can replace < *missing expression* >?

I. `(PetDog)map.get(honey.getName())`

II. `((PetDog)map.get(honey)).getBreed()`

III. `((PetDog)map.get(honey.getName())).getBreed()`

(A) I only
(B) II only
(C) I and II
(D) II and III
(E) I, II, and III

19.[AB] Which of the following code segments will compile with no errors and produce an alphabetical list of all three pets:

```
Honey -- Cocker Spaniel
Lucie -- Springer Spaniel
Murray -- Golden Retriever
```

I.

```
Set set = new TreeSet();
set.add(honey);
set.add(lucie);
set.add(murray);
Iterator iter = set.iterator();
while (iter.hasNext())
  System.out.println(iter.next());
```

II.

```
Map map = new TreeMap();
map.put(honey.getName(), honey);
map.put(lucie.getName(), lucie);
map.put(murray.getName(), murray);
Iterator iter = map.values().iterator();
while (iter.hasNext())
  System.out.println(iter.next());
```

III.

```
Map map = new HashMap();
map.put(honey.getName(), honey);
map.put(lucie.getName(), lucie);
map.put(murray.getName(), murray);
Iterator iter = map.keySet().iterator();
while (iter.hasNext())
  System.out.println(map.get(iter.next()));
```

(A) I only
(B) II only
(C) I and II
(D) II and III
(E) I, II, and III

20.[AB] `head1` points to the first node of a linked list that has three nodes with `Integer` values `0, 1, 2`; `head2` points to the first node of a list that has three nodes with `Integer` values `3, 4, 5`. What is the output from the following code?

```
ListNode node;
if (head1 != null && head2 != null)
{
  node = head1.getNext();
  head1.setNext(head2.getNext());
  head2.setNext(node);
}

for (node = head1; node != null; node = node.getNext())
  System.out.print(node.getValue() + " ");
for (node = head2; node != null; node = node.getNext())
  System.out.print(node.getValue() + " ");
```

(A) 0 1 2 3 4 5
(B) 0 4 5 3 1 2
(C) 3 4 5 0 1 2
(D) 3 0 2 0 4 5
(E) 3 0 1 2 4 5

21.[AB] What is the contents of the stack s1 (its elements listed starting from the top) after the following code is executed?

```
Stack stk = new ArrayStack();
Stack stk1 = new ArrayStack();
Stack stk2 = new ArrayStack();

int n;
Integer obj;
for (n = 1; n <= 6; n++)
  stk.push(new Integer(n));

while (!stk.isEmpty())
{
  obj = (Integer)stk.pop();
  n = obj.intValue();
  if (n % 2 != 0)
    stk1.push(obj);
  else
    stk2.push(obj);
}
while (!stk1.isEmpty())
  stk.push(stk1.pop());

while (!stk2.isEmpty())
  stk.push(stk2.pop());
```

(A) 1, 2, 3, 4, 5, 6
(B) 6, 5, 4, 3, 2, 1
(C) 1, 3, 5, 2, 4, 6
(D) 2, 4, 6, 1, 3, 5
(E) None of the above

22.[AB] Consider the following method:

```
public boolean someProperty(TreeNode root)
{
  return root != null &&
         (root.getLeft() != null && root.getRight() != null ||
              someProperty(root.getLeft()) ||
              someProperty(root.getRight()));
}
```

This method returns `true` if and only if the tree pointed to by `root`

(A) is not empty.
(B) is not empty and the root is not a leaf.
(C) is not empty and the root is either a leaf or has two children.
(D) has at least one node with two children.
(E) is a full tree.

23.[AB] The method `max(TreeNode root)` assumes as a precondition that `root` points to a non-empty binary search tree containing `Comparable` objects. `max` returns the value from the tree's largest node. Which of the following three versions of `max` return the correct answer when the precondition is met?

I.
```
public Object max(TreeNode root)
{
  while (root.getRight() != null)
    root = root.getRight();
  return root.getValue();
}
```

II.
```
public Object max(TreeNode root)
{
  Object maxValue = root.getValue();
  if (root.getRight() != null)
  {
    Object temp = max(root.getRight());
    if (((Comparable)temp).compareTo(maxValue) > 0)
      maxValue = temp;
  }
  return maxValue;
}
```

III.
```
public Object max(TreeNode root)
{
  Object maxValue = root.getValue();

  if (root.getLeft() != null &&
            ((Comparable)max(root.getLeft())).
                                compareTo(maxValue) > 0)
    maxValue = max(root.getLeft());

  if (root.getRight() != null &&
            ((Comparable)max(root.getRight())).
                                compareTo(maxValue) > 0)
    maxValue = max(root.getRight());

  return maxValue;
}
```

(A) I only
(B) II only
(C) I and II
(D) II and III
(E) I, II, and III

24. Given

```
int[] a = {1, 3, 5, 7, 9, 11, 13};
```

what are the values in `a` after `disarray(a, 7)` is called? The method `disarray` is defined as follows:

```
public void disarray(int[] a, int n)
{
  if (n > 1)
  {
    disarray(a, n-1);
    a[n-1] += a[n-2];
  }
}
```

(A) 1, 4, 9, 16, 25, 36, 49
(B) 1, 4, 8, 12, 16, 20, 24
(C) 1, 8, 12, 16, 20, 24, 13
(D) 1, 24, 20, 16, 12, 8, 4
(E) None of the above

25. The method `mixup` is defined as follows:

```
String mixup(String word)
{
  if (word.length() == 1)
    return "";
  else
    return mixup(word.substring(0, word.length() - 1))
                                 + word.charAt(word.length() - 2);
}
```

What is the value of the string returned by `mixup("IDEAL")`?

(A) `IDEAL`
(B) `IDEA`
(C) `LEAD`
(D) `LEDA`
(E) `DEAL`

2005

Answers and Solutions

1. C	6. B	11. B	16. D	21. B
2. D	7. B	12. D	17. A	22. B
3. C	8. A	13. B	18. C	23. E
4. E	9. C	14. D	19. C	24. C
5. E	10. A	15. E	20. A	25. E

1. Java is platform-independent.

2. `"1" + new Integer(2) + 3` is processed as
`("1" + String.valueOf(new Integer(2))) + 3`

3. `!(a || b)` is the same as `!a && !b`. `(!a && b) == (!a && !b)` if and only if `!a` is `false`, that is `a` is `true`.

4. The `java.util.Comparator` interface specifies the method
`public int compare(java.lang.Object,java.lang.Object)`.

5. All three options work. Option II works because `Test2005` extends `Year2005` and inherits its `toString` method. Option III works because `this` is a reference to the `Test2005` object whose `print` method is executing.

6. `a[0] = a[(0+3)%5] = a[3] = 1; a[1] = a[(2+3)%5] = a[0] = 1.`

7. If the length of a string is an odd number, greater or equal to 3, `mystery` reverses the center three-character substring and leaves the rest unchanged.

8. After the first `println`, `list` contains three strings, `"["`, `"A"`, and `"]"`. The first time through the `while` loop, the `if` condition calls `it.next()` once, due to short-circuit evaluation. `it.remove()` removes `"["`. The second time through the loop, the `if` condition calls `it.next()` twice. `it.remove()` removes the last accessed element, which is `"]"`. `"A"` alone remains in the list.

9. `insert` is not a method in `ArrayList`. The correct method is
`add(int i, Object x)`.

10. `ClassB` inherits both `methodA()` and `methodB()` from `ClassA`.

11. `ClassA`'s definition does not state that `ClassA` implements `InterfaceB`, even though `ClassA` has a method `methodB()`. Therefore, an object of `ClassA` is not an object of the `InterfaceB` type.

12. It is evident from the nested `for` loops that `rows` holds the number of rows in the rotated array, which is the number of columns, `a[0].length`, in the original array.

13. For example, `b[0][0]` gets its value from `a[0][2]`.

14. In one iteration, $n = 6$ or $n = 5$ becomes $n = 4$; $n = 4$ becomes $n = 3$; $n = 3$ remains $n = 3$. With enough iterations (e.g., 50), n eventually gets the value of 3 and stays there.

15. The `cities.add` call within the `for` loop increments the size of the `cities` list by one.

16. Static methods belong to a class as a whole and have no access to instance variables of individual objects.

17. The values `a[i] - b[i]` form an ascending sequence; we can work with these values using Binary Search. (There is no need to store these values in a temporary array: we can simply calculate them as necessary).

18. In a map, only one value can be associated with a given key. On the other hand, the same value can be associated with different keys. Therefore, each iteration through the `for` loop adds exactly one key-value pair to the map.

19. As the base case suggests, `mysteryProcess` removes all leaves from the tree.

20. `stk.push(stk)` places on the top of the stack a reference to the stack itself. When the first object is popped from the stack, it is an instance of `Stack`, so the `while` loop under `if (obj instanceof Stack)` is executed. It empties the stack, printing `"BA"`. Since the stack is left empty, the code jumps out of the outer `while` loop.

21.

```
                                 A          A           A           A
          A       A             / \        / \         / \         / \
M →      /   →   / \   →      G    N  →  G    N  →   G    E  →   G    E
        M       M   N        /           /\          /\   /       /\   /\
                            M           M  O        M  O N       M  O N  S
```

22. In Insertion Sort, the number of comparisons will not exceed $n + 5n$. Selection Sort and Mergesort are not equipped to take advantage of this situation.

23. Options I and II are straightforward; Option III works due to polymorphism.

24. `compareTo` uses `nuts`, while `hashCode` and `equals` use `bolts`. Different criteria for equal objects will be used in a `TreeSet` and `HashSet`, so the number of eliminated "duplicates" may be different when we add all objects from the list to `tSet` and `hSet`.

25. The best strategy is to choose E in all questions, which will yield 15 correct answers.

2004

Answers and Solutions

1. E	6. A	11. E	16. C	21. C
2. B	7. D	12. E	17. D	22. A
3. C	8. D	13. C	18. B	23. A
4. C	9. C	14. B	19. E	24. B
5. A	10. D	15. D	20. B	25. A

1. `twist` swaps the first characters in `words[0]` and `words[1]`.

2. A `Puzzle` is not always a kind of `Crossword`.

3. After the first two `add` calls, the list holds `Integer` objects with values 1 and 2. The third `add` inserts a reference to the second element (2) at the beginning of the list. Now the list holds 2, 1, 2, where the first and the last elements refer to the same object. So `x` and `y` refer to the same `Integer` object with the value 2.

4. The loop invariant condition must hold before the loop, after each iteration, and after the loop.

5. The binary representation of `p` changes from `00...001` to `00...010`, `00...100`, ... , `10...000`, after which it becomes 0. The binary representation of `sum` changes from `00...000` to `00...001`, `00...011`, ... `11...111`, after which it remains `11...111`, which represents –1.

6. The call

```
scramble(barb);
```

does not change `barb` because strings are immutable. To change `barb` we need

```
barb = scramble(barb);
```

7. The loop builds the Fibonacci sequence in `arr`.

8. `(int)(2 + 5 + 2.5 - 10 - 2/50)` is `(int)(-0.5 - 2/50)`, which gives 0.

9. 3 % 1 = 0; 4 % 2 = 0;
5 % 3 = 2; 6 % 4 = 2; ...; 10 % 8 = 2

10. The first removed value is at index 3. It is `word4`. After that, the indices shift to the left by one. The second removed value is at index 6, which is now `word8`.

11. The concept of privacy applies to the class as a whole, not to individual objects. The `hit` method can access and modify private fields in all objects of the `Particle` class.

12. `!(hours < hours0 || (hours == hours0 && mins < mins0))`

    Applying De Morgan's Laws, we get

    ```
    hours >= hours0 && (hours != hours0 || mins >= mins0)
    ```

13. Only Choice III correctly defines the `compareTo` method specified by the `Comparable` interface.

14. Only Choice II works, because `Gambler` does not have a no-args constructor. Choice I calls `Gambler`'s no-args constructor implicitly, so it is basically the same as Choice III.

15. Due to polymorphism, `liveAnotherDay` calls `CompulsiveGambler`'s `work` and `play` methods. `work` does nothing. `play` repeatedly calls `Gambler`'s `play`, which reduces the remaining amount of money by half, until 1 is left.

16. `goFigure(100)` returns 99. `goFigure(90)` returns 99 – 1 = 98. `goFigure(80)` returns 98 – 1 = 97. And so on.

17. When the first `"*"` is found, the second call to `it.next()`, within `it.add`, retrieves the next value in the list, which is `"B"`. `"*"` is appended to it, giving `"B*"`. Then `it.add` inserts `"B*"` after the last retrieved value (i.e., after `"B"`). We get `[A, *, B, B*, ...]`.

18. The statement

    ```
    head = doSomething(sort(head.getNext()), head);
    ```

    suggests that `doSomething(ListNode head, ListNode x)` inserts `x` into a sorted list, pointed to by `head`, and returns the head of the new list. We don't even have to look at `doSomething`'s code.

19. Get the next key, get the associated value, cast it into `Set`, remove `"Golf"` from that set.

20. The tree, built in the first seven lines and pointed to by `root`, looks like

```
        1
       / \
      /   \
     2     3
      \   / \
       4 5   6
```

The `toArray` method stores the values in an array using level-by-level left-to-right traversal, similar to representing a complete binary tree (e.g., a heap) in an array, with the first element unused.

21. A bucket in the `HashSet` implementation will hold on average 10 zip codes, and it will take, on average, 5 comparisons to find a target in its bucket. The BST in the `TreeSet` implementation will have the depth of 12, and it will take, on average, 11 or 12 comparisons to find a target.

22. This question contrasts mutable queues with immutable strings. In the `for` loop, the letters from the array `letters` are accumulated in two ways: a letter is added to a queue `qLetters` and appended to a string `sLetters`. On each iteration both `qLetters` and `sLetters` objects are saved on a stack. However, a reference to the same queue `qLetters` is saved on the stack, while `sLetters` changes, so a reference to a different string is saved on the stack. The `while(!stk.isEmpty())` loop on each iteration prints first the saved cumulative string then the queue. The queue is printed within `[ ]`. However, the first time we print the queue, we empty it. The subsequent iterations pop a reference to the same queue, which is now empty.

23. If we (logically) traverse the array in a snakewise manner, starting in the upper left corner, going down the first column, then up the second column, and so on, we get a sorted list with n^2 elements. We can always calculate the row and column for the k-th element in this logical list without actually building the list. Binary Search applies, so we can find a target value in $O(\log(n^2)) = O(2\log n) = O(\log n)$ time.

24. We need a constructor with two `int` arguments and a `moveBy` method. The `distanceFrom` method is inherited from `CartesianPoint`.

25. If b, c, d, or e is true, then a must be true, too. Therefore, b, c, d, and e must be false and a must be true.

2003

Answers and Solutions

1. D	6. B	11. D	16. A	21. A
2. C	7. D	12. C	17. D	22. D
3. B	8. C	13. C	18. B	23. A
4. E	9. C	14. C	19. E	24. B
5. E	10. A	15. D	20. E	25. B

1. `fun(v)` returns 4, so `v[0]` is set to 4.

2. `xProperty` returns `true` if `a` is equal to twice the sum of its digits.

3. $m + n = 22$ is the loop invariant here; m is incremented by 1 and n is decremented by 1 after every two iterations. Therefore at the end m is incremented by 10 and n is decremented by 10.

4. Choices B and C may result in `ArrayIndexOutOfBoundsException`. Choices A and D have the condition written incorrectly.

5. All three options work. A cast to `int` truncates a positive number towards zero.

6. Choice B corresponds exactly to the problem statement.

7. Starting from the second row and going down, the code "fills" a pixel with an `x` if both diagonal neighbors above it are `x`'s.

8. `"ONION".substring(1,5)` gives `"NION"`; `"NION".substring(1,4)` gives `"ION"`; `"ION".substring(0,3)` gives `"ION"` again.

9. For three values it is necessary and sufficient to compare each pair. For four values, first order any three of them using three comparisons, then compare the fourth with the one in the middle and use the fifth comparison to finish the ordering. For example, once you have established that $a \le b \le c$, compare d to b. If $d \le b$, then compare d to a; otherwise compare d to c.

10. The method searches for three consecutive elements whose values add up to `targetSum`. Each iteration of the `while` loop updates `sum` for the next triplet. Here no three consecutive values have the sum equal to 9.

11. You can build an oscillating array with arbitrary values in odd positions. Finding a minimum or a median in such an array takes as much time as in a random array.

12. Follow the contour of the blob, starting, say, in the lower left corner, adding the current column number (plus one) each time you go up.

13. Option I is standard. Option II works because `IncomingCall` has a no-args constructor. If it didn't, only Option I would be acceptable. Option III doesn't work because `tel` is private in `IncomingCall`.

14. `calls[0]` is an `IncomingCall` but not an `IncomingCallWithName`. An attempt to cast an object into a class type to which that object does not belong causes a `ClassCastException`.

15. `toString` is redundant in `IncomingCallWithName` because the `toString` method inherited from `IncomingCall` appropriately calls `IncomingCallWithName`'s `getSource` (due to polymorphism).

16. Choice B won't compile because `toString` is not defined in `Call`; Choice C fails to compile because `getName` is not defined in `Call`; Choice D fails for $i = 1$ with a `ClassCastException`.

17. `calls.remove(i)` adjusts the indices of subsequent values in the list, so `i` should not be incremented when a value is removed. Thus Option 1 fails to remove every other consecutive occurrence of `target`.

18. The code iterates over all the keys in the map (`"La"`, `"La-La"`, and `"La-La-La"`, in lexicographical order) and displays the values associated with them (`"La"`, `"La"`, and `"Ye-Ye"`, respectively).

19. This code segment removes consecutive duplicate values from the list.

20. This method returns the count of all the leaves plus all the nodes whose left and right child hold equal values.

21. The last node in the list is never added to the tree. You can prove that by using mathematical induction.

22. The resulting list must represent a path from the root of the tree to a leaf.

23. This method builds a Binary Search Tree. Inorder traversal of such a tree returns the values in ascending order.

24. `eval` uses a stack to evaluate a postfix expression (concatenating strings). Only Choice B offers a valid postfix expression.

25. Randy cannot get exactly 24 right because if 24 answers are correct, the 25th must be correct, too.

2002

Answers and Solutions

1. B	6. D	11. E	16. C	21. D
2. A	7. D	12. B	17. A	22. C
3. C	8. E	13. E	18. D	23. E
4. D	9. A	14. B	19. A	24. B
5. C	10. B	15. E	20. C	25. E

1.
```
x[0] + x[1] = 7 + 13 = 20
x[0] = (int)(700.0 / 20) = 35
x[0] + x[1] = 35 + 13 = 48
x[1] = (int)(1300.0 / 48) = 27
```

2. Consider a hypothesis: `isProcessedX` always leaves `v` unchanged and returns `false`. This is true for $n < 2$. If this hypothesis is true for $n-1$, it is also true for n. Hence it is true for any n. (This proof relies on the principle of mathematical induction.)

3. `property` is set to `false` if any value in an odd position is greater than or equal to one of its neighbors. In Choices A, B, D, and E, `mix[1]` satisfies this condition.

4. `board[0][1]`, `board[1][2]`, `board[2][3]`, and `board[3][0]` are set to `'x'`.

5. This method moves the last character in the first half of the string to the beginning and the first character in the second half of the string to the end. Then it applies recursively to the middle segment, excluding these two characters. The result is that both the first half of the string and the second half of the string are reversed.

6. `b` doubles after each two iterations, so in the end it ends up being multiplied by 32.

7. Choices A, B, C, and E give a wrong result for `weekDay` = 5 (and `weekDay` = 6).

8. Choice E is false, for example, for `v[] = {0, -1, 2, -1, 0.5, 0.5, 0.5, 0}`.

9. `x == a[i]` if and only if `x - a[0]` is a multiple of `a[1] - a[0]`.

10. `r` is a random number from 0 to `bigNum - 1`. In Choices A and E, `x` is always set to `arr[0]`. In Choice C, `arr[2]` is chosen slightly less frequently than `arr[0]` and `arr[1]`. Choice D fails when `r = 0`.

11. All three options work.

12. A `Person` cannot be assigned to a `SoccerPlayer` because `Person` is not a subclass of `SoccerPlayer` — it's the other way around.

13. This code compiles and runs. The question is which `compareTo` method will be called. Note that the `compareTo` in `SoccerPlayer` does not override `compareTo` in `Person`, because their parameters have different types. Either method potentially applies in this situation (because `SoccerPlayer` is an `Object`). In this situation Java ignores polymorphism and chooses the `compareTo` defined for `Person`, the explicitly stated type. `Person`'s `compareTo` compares names and returns `'M' - 'K'`.

14. `kristine.score()` increments `numGoals` in the `kristine` object even though it is already in the `team` set. The second `team.add(kristine)` has no effect because `kristine` is already in the set.

15. The original code does not work as expected when `players[k]` is already in the `mvps` list and is the first element in that list. In that case, `maxGoals` is obtained after the score of `players[k]` has been incremented. Any one of the three options corrects this problem.

16. To empty a list in Java, just discard it to the garbage collector and create a new empty list.

17. Use Binary Search to find the maximum (the place where `a[i] > a[i-1]` and `a[i] > a[i+1]`). Once the maximum is found, merge the two sorted parts of the array into one sorted array.

18. It may appear at first that we are trying to add the same object `str` to `set` three times. However, this is not so. Recall that `String`s are immutable. So `str += x` in fact discards the old string to which `str` refers and assigns the result of concatenation to `str`.

19. `p2` "moves" twice as fast as `p1`, so it must catch up with `p1` at some point. But `p2` cannot skip `p1`. If `p2` is one step behind, on the next step they will overlap.

20. The code scans `expr` from left to right and looks for matching pairs of parentheses. Once a matching pair is found, the code prints whatever is inside.

21. The method removes all the dots from the string and replaces any contiguous block of `x`'s or `o`'s with one `x` or `o`, respectively. The string in Choice D is packed to `"xoxox"`.

22. The values of `r` and `c` return to 0, 0 after 16 iterations.

23. Each node at the k-th level is visited 2^k times (assuming the root is at level 0). Here the node A is visited once, B and C twice each, D, E, and F four times each and G eight times.

24. The method adds an `"X"` in place of each missing child (when the other child is present).

25. If the exam has 8 easy questions, followed by 13 hard questions, followed by 3 easy questions, Skip will get 21 questions while Constance will get only 20.

2001

Answers and Solutions

1. E	6. B	11. B	16. C	21. D
2. C	7. D	12. A	17. A	22. C
3. E	8. A	13. C	18. B	23. D
4. A	9. C	14. E	19. A	24. B
5. B	10. D	15. E	20. E	25. A

1. `a` = 1 + 2 + 3 = 6; `b` = 2 + 6 + 3 = 11; `c` = 3 + 6 + 11 = 20

2. `g(x)` = `g(1)` = 2; `f(g(x))` = `f(2)` = 4
   `f(x)` = `f(1)` = 3; `g(f(x))` = `g(3)` = 6
   `x` = `x` + 4 - 6 = 1 + 4 - 6 = -1

3. We start with y = 0. Each iteration in the `while` loop takes the rightmost digit from `x` and appends it to `y` at the right. So `y` changes from 0 to 3 to 32 to 321.

4. When the center square `b[1][1]` is 'x', `xWon` checks only the four lines that go through the center square and fails to detect a winning configuration in the leftmost column.

5. In the `divide5(x,y,y)` call, `a[0]` is set to 21 and both `q` and `r` refer to the same array `y`. So the second statement in the method is the last one that sets the value of `y[0]`; it is set to 21 `%` 5 = 1.

6. `fun` increments those elements in the matrix whose indices are pairs of consecutive characters in `s`. The program prints the sum of the elements on the diagonal. This sum is equal to the number of times when two consecutive characters in `s` are the same.

7. After the loop, `!(k < n && a[k] >= 0)` must be true. Due to De Morgan's Laws, it is the same as `k >= n || a[k] < 0`.

8. `s` contains three or more of the same characters in a row if and only if (1) it has at least three characters and (2) either the first three characters in `s` are the same or the substring of `s` starting from the second character has three or more of the same characters in a row. This is formally stated in the recursive `xyz` method.

9. Consider `a = {3, 2, 1}`. In Options I and II, the first `if` inside the `for` loop will swap 2 and 3, but after that 2 will remain the first element in `a` and there will be no way to move it. So the array cannot be sorted. Option III sorts `a` correctly.

10. Insertion Sort, on average, is a quadratic sort — $O(n^2)$. So only Choices C, D, and E should be considered. The modified algorithm needs on average log n comparisons (in Binary Search) for each of the n elements. Besides, Choice C is nonsense and Choice E is impossible because $O(n)$ sorts based on comparisons do not exist.

11. The ball follows a figure-eight path starting at the center and completing the cycle in 16 moves:

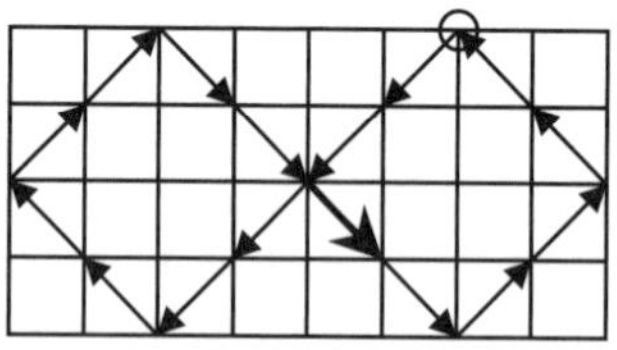

After 64 moves it is back in the center with the same direction. After that, six more moves take it to $x = 6$, $y = 4$.

12. Each x and y coordinate is incremented or decremented by one in each move. Therefore the sum of the coordinates cannot change from odd to even or from even to odd. It is initially 9/2 + 4/2 = 6. So it can't end up at 6 + 1 = 7.

13. A *loop invariant* must be true before the loop and at the end of each iteration through the loop. Also, it must have something to do with what the loop is trying to accomplish. Choices A, D, and E are not necessarily true before the loop, and Choice B is not true after the last iteration.

14. The method says that to make a valid word of length n, you can take any valid word of length $(n-1)$ and append 'B' or take any valid word of length $(n-2)$ and append "BA". Note that words formed using the first method end with a 'B' and words formed with the second method end with an 'A', so these two sets do not intersect. Therefore, if $f(n)$ is the number of valid words of length n, then $f(n) = f(n-1) + f(n-2)$. Actually, $f(n)$ are Fibonacci numbers! $f(0) = 1$ (empty word) and $f(1) = 2$, so $f(7) = 34$.

15. All three fragments correctly append the head node to `p`, set `next` in `head` to `null` and update `head`.

16. The first path through the `for` loop counts all cards in `hand` that are equal to the top one and pushes those that are not equal onto `stk`. The second path through the `for` loop again counts all the cards equal to the top one; all of them should be. The first and the second counts must be close to each other. Therefore, the method returns true if the hand is a "full house" — two cards of one rank and three cards of another rank.

17. First, using Binary Search on the top row, find the position of the last column that has black pixels. Then, again, using Binary Search on that column, find the last black pixel in it. Each of the two searches is $O(\log n)$, so the total is $O(\log n)$.

18. Since the `Point` class does not have a no-args constructor, a constructor in every subclass of `Point` must first call `super(x, y)`.

19. Lines 3 and 4 are valid because a `MovingPoint` IS-A `Point`, so `p2` can be passed as an argument to the `MovingPoint` constructor.

20. `MovingPoint` is a "wrapper" class for `Point`. `mp` "wraps around" `p`, and method calls for `mp` are channeled to `p`. So when `mp` moves, so does `p` embedded in it.

21. The left segment adds five different points to the set. Even though only three of them have different hash codes, the hash table resolves collisions properly. The right segment adds the same point five times to the set. The calls to `move` change the object already in the set. Normally the object would be added only the first time and the other calls to `add` would have no effect, because duplicates are not allowed in a set. However, in the `HashSet` implementation, `hashCode` is called first and may return different values as the point moves. Thus `p` may be placed into different buckets and the `HashSet` fails to detect that `p` is already in the set. Here three references to the same object `p` end up in three different buckets.

22. Both `p1` and `p2` wrap around the same point `p`. When this point moves, both `p1` and `p2` move, too, even when they are already placed into the queue.

23. The method doesn't do anything to a tree with a single node and returns 0. It returns `-1` for any other tree. Therefore, if both `root.getLeft()` and `root.getRight()` are leaves, then `magic(root.getLeft())` and `Magic(root.getRight())` do nothing and their sum is `0`. After the condition `if (sum == 0)` is checked, the `root.getLeft()` and `root.getRight()` are swapped. Otherwise, `magic` is performed on the left and right subtrees, swapping leaves with a common parent in each of them.

24. After `traversePreOrder`, stack holds (from top to bottom) `GFCEDBA`. `traversePostOrder` makes

left subtree *right subtree* *root*

```
    C          B         A
   / \        / \
  G   F      E   D
```

25. Since I and III enter symmetrically in possible answers (a) - (e), Choices B and D, which break the symmetry, should be eliminated. So the real question is: Should she start with I or II? If she starts with I, the following decision tree results:

```
                        I
                       / \
                   F /     \ T
                    /        \
remaining       II only      I only
possibilities:  III only     I and II
                II and III
```

On the right branch one test (II) resolves it and on the left branch there is a 50% chance that a second test will be necessary (if the first one gives true). If she starts with II, the following decision tree results:

```
                       II
                      /  \
                  F /      \ T
                   /         \
remaining       I only       II only
possibilities:  III only     I and II
                             II and III
```

This tree is symmetrical to the one above. Here on the left branch one test resolves it and on the right branch a second test may be needed with 50% probability. Either way, the average path to a complete solution has the same length whether we start with I or II.

2000

Answers and Solutions

1. C	6. D	11. C	16. E	21. B
2. A	7. C	12. D	17. D	22. B
3. B	8. E	13. B	18. E	23. E
4. C	9. E	14. C	19. A	24. A
5. A	10. C	15. B	20. A	25. D

1. Integer division truncates `2/3` to 0.

2. Since at the beginning `arr[k]` is equal to `k` for `k` = 0, ..., 4, it remains unchanged.

3. The clue is Choice E: it says `c` and `d` are not the same. Choice A says one and not the other is true, Choice C says at least one is true and at least one is false, Choice D says at least one but not both are true. Choice B says a wrong thing: both `!c` and `!d` must be true.

4. Within the loop a number is replaced six times by its square. This is the same as raising it to the 64-th power. So the result must be close to *e*.

5. The elements of `counts` are initialized to 0 when the array is created. The inner loop increments `counts[0]` by 4 (it is incremented for `j` = 0, 3, 6, and 9) and `counts[1]` and `counts[2]` by 3. The outer loop repeats it 100 times, so at the end `counts[0]` is 400 and `counts[1]` and `counts[2]` are 300 each. The output statement uses integer division, so 600/400 is truncated to 1.

6. The values in the array are 0, 1, 1, 0, -1, -1, 0, 1, 1, and so on.

7. The first iteration of the outer `for` loop saves `'G'` in `temp`, then sets `s.charAt(1)` to `s.charAt(0)`, `s.charAt(2)` to `s.charAt(1)`, and so on, resulting in all `'W'`s, then sets `s.charAt(0)` to `'G'`. The overall result is `"GWWWWWW"`. The other two outer iterations work with all `'W'`s and do not change the result.

8. Each call to the method with $n > 1$ adds one star. The sequence of calls is $n = 5, 6, 3, 4, 2$, and 1.

9. It is OK to concatenate a `String` with an `Integer` — the result is a `String`. The `String.valueOf(x)` method is used to convert `x` into a `String` when necessary. A less obvious fact is that `String.valueOf(null)` returns `"null"`.

10. The method fails to check that the stack is left empty at the end. It should say `return s.isEmpty()` rather than `return true`.

11. In Option I:

```
a[0] = 1 - 2*1*1 = -1              | d = 2;
a[1] = 1 - 2*(-1)*(-1) = -1        | a[0] -= 2; ==> a[0] = -1
                                   | a[1] -= 2; ==> a[1] = -1
```

In Option II:

```
a[0] = 1 - 2*1*0 = 1               | d = 0;
b[1] = 0 - 2*1*0 = 0               | a[0] -= 0; ==> a[0] = 1
                                   | b[1] -= 0; ==> b[1] = 0
```

In Option III:

```
a[0] = 1 - 2*1*1 = -1              | d = 2;
c[1] = 1 - 2*(-1)*1 = [3]          | a[0] -= 2; ==> a[0] = -1
                                   | c[1] -= 2; ==> c[1] = [-1]
```

12. 5 would be found right away in the middle. 1 and 21 would be found because they are the smallest and the largest and they are at the ends. 3 would be found on the second step because it is in the middle of the left segment.

13. For an array of $3 = 2^2 - 1$ elements, one comparison finds it (because we know the target is somewhere in the array). For $7 = 2^3 - 1$ elements, 2 comparisons may be necessary. For an array of $2^{12} - 1$ elements, it must be 11.

14. $x = 1$ is a good test: we should get 3 but Choice A gives 15, Choice B gives 5, and Choice D gives something close to 9. Choice E gives a negative number for $x = 6$.

15. `encrypt` first replaces `'x'` characters with the letters from the message, starting in the top row, going left to right, then in the second row, and so on. This alone eliminates Choices A, D, and E. Then it continues with the message. It scans the `key` matrix again, placing letters in places that are symmetrical to `'x'` characters with respect to the center of the matrix.

16. The *x*-coordinate of the leftmost point of the circle is `xCenter - radius`, so it is always 100 in `new Circle(x + 100, 100, x)`.

17. The picture is repeated in the same place but is scaled by a factor of two.

18. `expand` replaces `"0"` with `"01"` and `"1"` with `"10"`. Among other things, `expand("1001")` returns a string that has 8 characters, so the string returned by `expand(expand("1001"))` should have 16 characters.

19. The presence of the `toggle` and `isOn` methods does not in itself prove that `ToggleSwitch` implements `Toggleable`.

20. Options II and III fail to create the elements of `buttons`. This would cause a `NullPointerException`.

21. Option I has `push` calling itself and causing infinite recursion; Option III attempts to access a private field (`buttons`) of the superclass.

22. The method makes the picture thinner by removing all pixels whose two neighbors — above and to the left — are set to `'x'`. There are four such pixels in the original picture.

23. When the array is split into two halves and all the elements in the right half are greater than all the elements in the left half, `merge` is not called. This is the case here, as the array is first split into 2 1 3 4 and 6 5 8 7 and then these segments are further split into 2 1 / 3 4 and 6 5 / 8 7. When the array has only two elements, they are swapped, if necessary, and no recursive calls are made. So `merge` will be never called.

24. This method is a version of Quicksort in disguise. The first element removed from `q` is the pivot. Then all the elements that are less than or equal to the pivot are sent to `q1` and the rest are sent to `q2`. Then `q1` and `q2` are sorted recursively and finally collected back into `q` with the pivot between them.

25. Go from the bottom up marking the values of `xSum` for the corresponding subtree:

```
        12        (5+8-1=12)
       /  \
     1     8      (4+0-3=1;  2+13-7=8)
    /     / \
   3     7   13   (1+12-0=13)
               \
                12
```

1999

Answers and Solutions

1. A	6. B	11. C	16. C	21. E
2. E	7. D	12. A	17. D	22. D
3. C	8. C	13. E	18. D	23. E
4. B	9. A	14. D	19. C	24. A
5. A	10. B	15. A	20. B	25. B

1. `5/2` in integer division is 2. The cast to `double` applies to the result; 2 - 2 = 0.

2. `u += 5 ==> u = 8; v += 8 ==> v = 13; u -= 13 ==> u = -5;`
   `v -= -5 ==> v = 18`

3. `95/100` is truncated to 0.

4. `inc` is toggled between 1 and -1, so after an even number of iterations both `count1` and `count2` are 0. After the eleventh iteration `count1` becomes 1 and `count2` becomes -1.

5. A method `equals(int)` is not defined in the `Integer` class. It is `equals(Object)`.

6. Note no `break` in `case` 0. The values of `a`, `b`, and `a+b` coming into the switch and the outputs after the switch are as follows:

```
a    b    a+b  print(b)
------------------------
0    0    0       1
1    1    2       2
1    2    3       2
2    2    4       0
2    0    2       1
2    1    3       1
3    1
```

7. After the first iteration in the `while` loop, `n` becomes 31. The second iteration adds 21 and 1, so `n` becomes 53. After that, each iteration adds 4, until `n` reaches 93.

8. If `n` is not positive, that number is displayed. A positive `n` is incremented until it reaches 100, then displayed.

9. This is a trick question. At the last iteration through the second `for` loop, `i` and `j` become equal, and the middle element's value is subtracted from itself.

10. `Integer` objects are immutable, so `mysteryMix` cannot change their values.

11. `folder` is an `ArrayList`, so the correct way to access its *k*-th element is `folder.get(k)`. This method returns an `Object`. You need to cast `folder.get(k)` into `Index` to call methods of the `Index` class.

12. Options II and II may call `msg.getStatus` when `msg` is `null`, causing a `NullPointerException`.

13. Choices A and C call a constructor of the `Picture` class that does not exist. In Choice B, `picture` has the type `Drawable`, so the compiler does not know that `picture` has an `add` method. In Choice D, a private instance variable `pictures` is not accessible.

14. `box` is modified even after it is added to `picture`. `picture.draw(g)` draws all elements in its `pictures` list relying on polymorphism. In this case it draws two lines and a box. `box.draw(g)` in turn draws the four lines in its list.

15. `Box` inherits the appropriate versions of `draw` and `add` from `Picture`.

16. `picture` has one element in it, `box`, so the result must be `[Picture [Box ...]]`. `box` has six lines in it: four added in its constructor and two more added explicitly by the `add` calls. `box`'s name is displayed because `Picture`'s `toString` method polymorphically calls `Box`'s `getName`.

17. `picture` is added to its own list as an element. This compiles fine but causes a stack overflow due to infinite recursion when `picture.draw` calls `(picture.get(0)).draw()`, i.e., itself.

18. The code in Option I displays

```
Honey is a Honey -- Cocker Spaniel
```

In Option II, a `PetDog` object is used as a key rather than a `String`. Still, this works because `honey.hashCode()` and `honey.equals(name)` return the same results as `honey.getName().hashCode()` and `honey.getName().equals(name)`, respectively.

19. Option I works because set is a `TreeSet` and its iterator produces objects in ascending order. In Option II, we incorrectly use an iterator for the set of values rather than for the set of keys. Still, it works because in this case the order for the keys and the values is the same. In Option III we use a hash table and its iterator does not guarantee that the keys are scanned in any particular order.

20. The code swaps the segments of the lists that are attached to their heads. 4, 5 becomes attached to 0 and 1, 2 becomes attached to 3. Then it displays the values from the first list followed by the values from the second list.

21. After the first `for` loop, `stk` contains (from the top) 6, 5, 4, 3, 2, 1. After the first `while` loop, `stk` is empty, `stk1` holds 1, 3, 5, and `stk2` holds 2, 4, 6. After the two remaining `while` loops, `stk` holds 5, 3, 1, 6, 4, 2.

22. This answer fits because a tree has one node with two children if and only if it is not empty and at least one of the following is true: its root has two children, the left subtree has a node with two children, or the right subtree has a node with two children.

23. Since this is a binary search tree, the largest value is in the rightmost node of the tree. The code in Option I correctly finds that node. Option II uses recursion to find the largest value in the right subtree and compares it with the root. It works because we know that the largest value must be in the root or in the right subtree. Option III does not use the fact that this is a BST and is less efficient, but it works, too.

24. The method replaces `a[i]` with `a[0] + ... + a[i]`. This property is easy to prove using the principle of mathematical induction. The sum of the first several odd numbers is a perfect square, so Choice A is a plausible answer.

25. A plausible hypothesis is that `mixup` simply cuts off the last letter from the string. This is true when `word` has only one character: `mixup("A")` is `""`. According to the recursive method definition,

    `mixup("AB")` is `mixup("A") + 'A' = "" + 'A' = "A"`
    `mixup("ABC")` is `mixup("AB") + 'B' = "A" + 'B' = "AB"`
    And so on.

Index

Other Computer Science and Calculus Titles from Skylight Publishing

Be Prepared for the AP Computer Science Exam in Java
ISBN 0-9654853-5-8

Java Methods: An Introduction to Object-Oriented Programming
ISBN 0-9654853-7-4

Java Methods AB: Data Structures
ISBN 0-9654853-1-5

---

100 Multiple-Choice Questions in C++
ISBN 0-9654853-0-7

C++ for You++: An Introduction to Programming and Computer Science ISBN 0-9654853-9-0

Workbook to Accompany C++ for You++
ISBN 0-9654853-8-2

Be Prepared for the AP Calculus Exam
ISBN 0-9727055-5-4

800 Questions in Calculus
ISBN 0-9727055-4-6

Solutions to 800 Questions in Calculus
Part 0-9727055-C-D